D1457663

# Armenian History

*A Captivating Guide to the History of
Armenia and the Armenian Genocide*

# Free Bonus from Captivating History (Available for a Limited time)

Hi History Lovers!

Now you have a chance to join our exclusive history list so you can get your first history ebook for free as well as discounts and a potential to get more history books for free! Simply visit the link below to join.

Captivatinghistory.com/ebook

Also, make sure to follow us on Facebook, Twitter and Youtube by searching for Captivating History.

# Table of Contents

# Part 1: History of Armenia

*A Captivating Guide to Armenian History, Starting from Ancient Armenia to Its Declaration of Sovereignty from the Soviet Union*

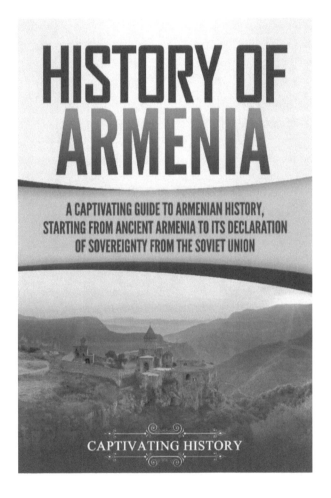

Here is a flag for you, my brother,

    that I have sewn by hand

    over the sleepless nights

    and bathed in my tears.

    - Armenian National Anthem

# Introduction

Humanity may have been born in the mountains of Armenia. Biblical accounts tell that it survived there, that after a terrible flood wiped out the human race, a group of people made a fresh start on the flanks of Mount Ararat. And survival has been the theme of this ancient nation's history, a story that is nothing short of epic and inspiring.

The tale of Armenia has its beginnings as a glorious ancient kingdom, one that commanded the respect of nations as mighty as Egypt and Babylonia. As its history takes a turn for the darker, each chapter reads like a roll call of the most famous of figures: Antony and Cleopatra, Alexander the Great, Genghis Khan, Frederick Barbarossa. Armenia saw ancient Rome rise to power; it knew Egyptian pharaohs, the Golden Horde, the Soviet Union, and saw the first invasion of the first Muslim army. For a long and ugly part of its history, Armenia struggled under the yokes of one empire after another: the Roman, Parthian, Persian, Byzantine, Timurid, Mongolian, and Ottoman Empires, to name just a few.

Yet through it all, Armenia, time and time again, emerged as a nation with a powerful identity, one that caused much grief over the years, but one that still remains a pillar of strength to its people in good times and in bad. There is much sorrow held within these pages; much oppression, much persecution, and even the most terrible evil of them all—genocide. The reading is made easy by one single gleaming light, a golden thread running through every word and chapter, and that light is the Armenian people themselves.

Their story is tragic, but their survival is incredible. And that is what makes their tale so inspiring.

# Chapter 1 – The Home of Eden

And a river went out of Eden to water the garden; and from thence it was parted, and became into four heads. The name of the first *is* Pison: that *is* it which compasseth the whole land of Havilah, where *there is* gold; And the gold of that land *is* good: there *is* bdellium and the onyx stone. And the name of the second river *is* Gihon: the same *is* it that compasseth the whole land of Ethiopia. And the name of the third river *is* Hiddekel: that *is* it which goeth toward the east of Assyria. And the fourth river *is* Euphrates.

- Genesis 2:10-14

For millennia, Christian scholars have searched for the Garden of Eden, the biblical home of the birth of mankind. These scholars speculate that one of the most likely locations for the home of Eden is in the heart of one of the most ancient countries in the world: Armenia. With four rivers flowing through its abundant landscape—including those still known today as the Tigris and Euphrates—Armenia is one of the oldest homes of the human race. To paraphrase the British admiral

John Byron, according to biblical beliefs, Adam was created from the dust of Armenia.

In fact, with its modern-day capital Yerevan nestled on the flanks of Mount Ararat, Armenia may be the biblical location not only of the birth of humankind but also one of rebirth: it was on Mount Ararat that Noah's ark was beached after the flood, according to scriptures.

Regardless of where that biblical garden may be located, it is certain that Armenia has been home to humanity for many, many thousands of years.

* * * *

5,500 years ago—around 3500 BCE—a lonely figure strode across the soaring landscapes of his ancient paradise. Surrounded by the towering walls of mountain peaks, the man paused on the rocky hilltop, gazing at the majesty of the surrounding countryside. Rivers and lakes were splashes of blue in the valleys below; the icy wind combed the waving grass of the harsh mountainside where the man stood. Around him, a flock of sheep picked at the grass, seeking out sustenance where they could in this beautiful, bleak landscape.

Their shepherd had a mane of scarlet hair that tossed in the cold breeze. It was a splash of fire among the more neutral colors of the surroundings, and it crowned a figure that looked different from the people of today, one that was shorter and more powerfully built. The young man's eyes were piercing as he gazed out across the mountainous region where he had made his home. He shifted his weight, feeling his feet safely encased inside the leather shoes that covered them. Other peoples of the age wore sandals, but in the chill of the mountains, closed shoes were essential.

The red-haired man paused only for a moment before heading off again, summoning his sheep and moving purposefully across the flank of the mountain. And little did he know that his simple leather shoe—made from cowhide and carefully sewn into shape—would be discovered 5,500 years later and make history as the oldest shoe ever discovered.

Known as the Areni-1 shoe, this ancient piece of footwear, which is older than Stonehenge, was found in a cave complex near the modern-day village of Areni, Armenia. It was a testimony to the Chalcolithic period, a transitional period between the Stone Age and the Bronze Age, and the people that have lived in this ancient country for so many years. Perfectly preserved in layers of droppings from the sheep that ancient Armenians kept, it was even stuffed with grass, possibly in an attempt to keep its shape. The Chalcolithic period featured the first use of metal, giving it the colloquial name of the Copper Age—a somewhat poetic name, considering that DNA found in the same caves as the shoe indicated that at least one of the cave's ancient inhabitants had red hair and blue eyes.

Little is known of these ancient Armenians, and even less is known of the other cultures around that period, but we do know that humans have been living there for a very long time. The Areni-1 cave complex gave rise to numerous important discoveries from even before the time of our redheaded shepherd. Burial sites that were from as many as 6,000 years ago have been discovered there since the excavation began by an Irish-Armenian team in 2007; for example, a skull from a preteen, found in a clay pot, yielded a sample of amazingly well-preserved brain tissue from the Stone Age. There was even a winepress in those caves, making it the oldest winery ever discovered. In fact, the shoes we imagined on the feet of our shepherd may actually have been designed for trampling grapes to release their juice and turn it into an ancient alcoholic drink that we still enjoy today.

The Shulaveri-Shomu culture was one of the earliest known cultures to live in Armenia; they were around a little before our well-shod redhead, living there around 4000 BCE. These were followed by the

Bronze Age Kura-Araxes culture, named after one of the rivers where they made their home, the Araxes (whose name means "fast-flowing" or "dashing," the same as the name Gihon, mentioned in the biblical account of the Garden of Eden's location). Finally, the Trialeti-Vanadzor culture, existing around 1600 BCE, made their homes in Armenia and its surroundings, including modern-day Turkey and Georgia.

One of the very first ancient Armenians whom we know by name is a folk hero from about 2500 BCE—about a thousand years after the lifetime of the wearer of that ancient shoe. His story is so old and so steeped in tradition that his very existence is questionable. However, where archaeology has failed to discover the exact origins of the Armenian people, their traditions have, for centuries, traced back to a single hero: Hayk Nahapet.

* * * *

"Nahapet" means "patriarch" in Armenian, and Hayk is looked upon as the progenitor of all the Armenian people. According to tradition, he originally served Nimrod, a hunter, warrior, king, and the founder of Babylonia. A subject of the ancient empire of Babylon, Hayk grew tired of its new king, Bel, and emigrated to the shadow of Mount Ararat, where the bones of Noah's ark still rested on the mountaintop.

Founding a village that he named after himself, Hayk tried to settle down with his family, despite Bel's pleas for him to return. When Hayk continued to refuse to go back to Babylon, the petulant king turned angry. He marched on Hayk's village with a vast army, determined to raze Haykashen to the ground.

But Hayk would not be so easily cowed. He had learned in the shadow of Nimrod, a heroic warrior who had built the empire that Bel was abusing. He armed himself with a bow and gathered his army on the shores of Lake Van, and there, where the great lake lay like a pool of liquid glass among the sentinel figures of the mountains, the Battle of the

Giants took place.

When the Babylonians came pouring down the mountainside, Hayk was quick to spot Bel's hated visage among the churning mass of the vanguard. Stringing an arrow, he raised his bow, drawing it with his powerful arms. His glittering eyes focused on the chest of his great enemy, and even though the world rang with the battle cries of Babylonian and Haykashen citizens, Hayk heard nothing but the soft creak of his bow. He breathed out and fired the arrow. It lanced through the air, an impossibly long shot. It couldn't possibly make it. Hayk's tiny army was doomed in the face of the might of Babylonia.

Except it wasn't. True and fierce, the arrow arced through the air and plunged deep into Bel's heart. He collapsed, and his army was thrown into disarray. Hayk and his men rushed forward, and the defeat of the Babylonians was complete.

\* \* \* \*

The traditional date of the legendary Battle of Giants is August 11th, 2492 BCE. How much of the story is true is unknown; however, to this day, the Armenian word for an Armenian person is *hay*, and for Armenia, *Hayk!*

By 1446 BCE, the nation founded on Hayk's single arrow had become known as Hayastan, or the Hayasa-Azzi kingdom. It had risen in prominence to become one of the greatest of ancient powers, revered even by the Egyptian pharaoh of the time. Thutmose III was arguably the most powerful pharaoh of ancient Egypt, as he controlled the largest empire of any pharaoh, stretching all the way from Syria to Nubia after seventeen campaigns were launched to expand his territory. But Hayastan never fell to Thutmose's blade. He called it Ermenen, one of the earliest references to Armenia that resembles its modern English name, and wrote at length about its beauty. "Heaven rests upon its four pillars," he said.

By 1200 BCE, as the Bronze Age began to reach its end, the Hayasa-Azzi kingdom had faded from the pages of history. The former unity of the kingdom was gone, replaced by different tribes scattered across the face of Armenia, but the people still understood that there was power in standing together, even though their kingdom had fallen. A confederation of tribes was established in the Armenian highlands around that same lake where Hayk had made his fateful stand. This confederation was named "Nairi" ("Land of Rivers") by its greatest enemies, the neighboring and powerful Assyrians. Yet the Assyrians were unable to defeat the Nairi. Absorbing the peoples of the Hayasa-Azzi kingdom, the Nairi was a formidable force, strong enough to withstand the onslaught of both the Assyrians and the Hittites.

For the next four hundred years, the Nairi would be the glowing height of Armenian power. But the power to follow, a kingdom founded around the mountain where Noah's ark had landed, would prove to be even greater still.

# Chapter 2 – The Rise and Fall of Urartu

Considering that the Kingdom of Urartu was only really discovered by archaeologists in the 19$^{th}$ century CE, after having disappeared from history for almost a thousand years, it is unsurprising that the name might sound unfamiliar to the contemporary reader. Urartu was an Assyrian name for the great kingdom that was born from the womb of the Nairi, but its Hebrew name would be familiar to the modern ear: Ararat, the same as the biblical mountain at whose feet the kingdom grew up.

Those same Assyrians who named Urartu were the very threat that forced the Nairi to become more than just a confederation of tribes and petty little kingdoms. The Assyrian Empire—known as the first true empire in history—was one of the most formidable forces in the world at that point. Its last incarnation, the Neo-Assyrian Empire, was also its strongest; starting from 911 BCE, it proved to be almost impossible to defeat. Powers as great as Egypt and Jerusalem fell before its charging hordes of soldiers and chariots, and there was nothing that could stand against it.

Compared with the might of Jerusalem that had fallen almost entirely in the face of the Assyrians, the Nairi were nobodies. There was no way that their little confederation could hope to stand against Assyria—or at least, so it looked on paper. But there was a powerful leader determined to rise up against the marauding invaders, a man who was ready to do whatever it took to defend his people and his kingdom. And that man would become King Arame, the first king of Urartu.

Arame was a leader so powerful that he eventually became legendary. Armenian tradition likely bases one of its greatest heroes—Ara the Beautiful—on this first great king. Ara the Beautiful was a warrior so noble and handsome that he attracted the attentions of Semiramis, a sorceress. When Ara scorned her, Semiramis declared war on his kingdom, ordering her soldiers to capture Ara alive. Somehow, Ara was killed, and the distraught Semiramis raised him from the dead, causing the end of the war with his kingdom.

While it is unlikely that necromancy was part of Arame's true story, he was certainly a very capable leader since he managed to stand against the Assyrian king, Shalmaneser III. Forging the diverse group of tribes into a single united front ready to stand against the Assyrians, Arame was made the first king of the Nairi in 858 BCE. Under his leadership, the Nairi put up a spirited defense. Shalmaneser did succeed in capturing the capital, but their lands were not wholly defeated, and its rulers kept it from the clutches of Assyria for centuries to come.

Arame laid the foundation for a kingdom that would grow to become one of the greatest powers in the ancient Middle East. By the end of his rule, Armenia was no longer simply a confederation called the Nairi—it was a kingdom, the Kingdom of Urartu. He was succeeded by Sarduri I, whose ancestry is disputed; he may have been Arame's son, but some sources call him the son of Lutipri, therefore making him a usurper. Regardless of the legitimacy of Sarduri's claim to the throne, he followed in Arame's footsteps as a strong leader. Having lost the former capital of the kingdom to the Assyrians, Sarduri continued to work on unifying his people. He built a new capital in 830 BCE, laying its foundations on a limestone promontory on the eastern shore of Lake Van—the very place where the legendary Hayk had taken his stand against the enemy hordes.

The new city, named Tushpa, would later be known as Van. For now, however, its stone citadel was a stronghold that Sarduri hoped would be able to withstand the invading Assyrians. His hopes would come true; while Shalmaneser continued his attempts to invade Urartu, Sarduri's defenses were, for the most part, successful. Urartu was starting to find its way onto the map as the strange little kingdom that the Assyrians just could not beat.

Sarduri's successor, Ishpuini, took the throne after Sarduri's death in 828 BCE. Tushpa was just two years old at that point, but already, Urartu was feeling the effects of increased security throughout the land. In fact, Ishpuini was the first Urartian king who could turn his attention from defense to offense. He was, of course, not foolish enough to attack the Assyrians. Instead, he set his sights on an easier target: the city of Musasir. It is uncertain where exactly Musasir was located—an archaeological site near Lake Urmia in Iran is one of the potential locations—but the city and its surroundings bordered on Urartu, and Ishpuini wanted them. He annexed the city and then turned his attention to religion and culture instead of war. The Urartians had a unique polytheistic religion, and Ishpuini seemed to be a devoted follower. He made Musasir the religious center of Urartu and made regular pilgrimages there, introducing his people to the cult of Haldi, who was a warrior god who could have possibly been the Urartian god of the sun as well. Ishpuini was also the first Urartian king to keep his records in his native language.

King Menua, who co-ruled with Ishpuini, helped to expand the borders of the growing kingdom even farther. By the time he became the sole ruler in approximately 810 BCE, the kingdom was no longer known by its own name as the kingdom of the Nairi. Instead, it was given a new moniker: *Bianili*, or "from Biani," the Urartian name for the region around Lake Van.

The Assyrians were going through a period of stagnation themselves, and so, the Urartians were able to keep their focus on increasing their power rather than defending it. This led to a period of prosperity for the everyday people of Urartu, and they developed a fascinating and complicated culture. Like their ancestors from prehistoric times, the Urartians were winemakers and shepherds, but they were perhaps most gifted in raising horses. The rocky highlands held rich grazing for the animals that were strong and tough enough to climb the mountainsides to get to it; this led to the breeding of hardy horses that, when brought down from the mountains, had a greater lung capacity than their lowland cousins. They could outrun any Assyrian horse harnessed to a chariot, leading to a growing trade of horses between Urartu and Assyria in times of peace. The Urartians were also some of the earliest horsemen, riding astride their swift animals rather than riding only in chariots.

Art was another favorite occupation for the Urartians. They built extravagant temples, commonly using the limestone that was so profuse in the region, and decorated them with stone carvings and inscriptions, as well as painting on the plastered walls. Vibrant blues and reds were their favorite colors, and the Urartians depicted scenes from their lives and faith. They were also gifted metalworkers; everything from statues to hinges could be made out of bronze, and as the Iron Age dawned across civilization, Urartians soon learned these skills, too.

Under the rule of Argishti I in the 8th century BCE, Urartu reached the height of its power. Its borders encompassed parts of modern-day Armenia, Turkey, Georgia, and Iran, and it was a formidable power that rose up in a time when Assyria was crushing everything in its path. Yet even though it had once made peace with its oldest enemy, Urartu would fall victim to an Assyrian invasion. And this time, there would be no Arame to save it.

★ ★ ★ ★

King Rusa I of Urartu had been brought to the very brink of despair.

Tiglath-Pileser III, the same biblical Assyrian king who had terrorized the lands of Israel and Judah, had spent the early years of Rusa I's reign—in the late 8th century BCE—decimating Urartu. The Assyrian king had seized many of Urartu's lands and laid waste to both their cities and their economy before leaving the crippled kingdom a mere shadow of the great power it had been under Argishti I. And while Tiglath-Pileser III had died in 727 BCE, the period of rest that Urartu had experienced after his death turned out not to be a path to new prosperity but simply a breather. Sargon II ascended the throne in 722 BCE, and in 715 BCE, he set his sights on a nation that had been a thorn in the side of Assyria since its inception: Urartu.

The Urartu-Assyrian War had been raging for two long, hard, devastating years, having started in 714 BCE. Like all the Urartian kings before him, Rusa I had not relied on generals to lead his men into battle. Instead, he had been at the forefront of every fight, swinging his own sword into the butchering masses of the invaders, and he had personally witnessed one defeat after the other. Urartu's depleted resources were no match for Assyria at the height of its power, and Sargon II was sowing destruction everywhere he went.

To make matters even worse, the Cimmerians—nomads from the Caucasus—chose the year 714 BCE, the height of the war with Assyria, to attempt to invade Urartu. Rusa did his best to fight two wars at once, but it was clear that Urartu was being crushed between the scissor blades of two enemies, and it did not help that this was happening at the tail end of decades of oppression.

Now, Rusa was facing not only the threat of his enemies but also utter humiliation and the loss of a city that was at the very heart of the Urartian faith and people. The Battle of Mount Waush had been a rare victory for Rusa, and when he had routed Sargon and put his troops to flight, the king had begun to hope that perhaps the tide was turning. Maybe Urartu was going to make it out of this after all. But Sargon's pride had been deeply wounded by the way he had been forced to turn tail and run, and he was bent on getting his revenge on Rusa. There was no city that meant more to Rusa and his people than Musasir, and so, Sargon set the holy city of Urartu alight.

The news of Musasir's burning would have been to Rusa what it would have been for a Muslim to hear of the sacking of Mecca. It was a devastating blow, and one that was too much for a king who had already suffered desperately during his reign. Most of his years as king had been occupied in hopeless warfare, and Rusa knew he was watching his kingdom slide away into oblivion and that he was helpless to stop it. Faced with the despair of his people as their beloved city was torched to ashes, Rusa could not see any way out. So, he took his own weapon and killed himself.

With their king dead, the Urartians had little option but to negotiate a surrender with the Assyrians. They were forced to pay tribute to Assyria, which was a crippling amount considering the toll that years of warfare had taken on their failing economy.

Nevertheless, refusing to give up, Rusa's son, Argishti II, followed in the footsteps of his powerful namesake by attempting to restore Urartu to some semblance of the greatness it had enjoyed during the 9ᵗʰ century.

As Urartu limped into the 7ᵗʰ century BCE, Argishti managed to nurse the economy back to health, despite the tribute owed to Assyria, and Urartian culture managed to flourish in the face of adversity for another century. It was only around 612 BCE, when the Medes and the Scythians joined forces to conquer Assyria, that Urartu finally fell. The Medes invaded it and took its capital, by then known as Van, in 590 BCE.

Urartu was gone, but its people lived on, oppressed though they were by the Medes and the Scythians. Sadly for them, this was only their first taste of oppression. The centuries that followed would see a string of conquerors coming for the natural resources so richly present in Urartu, which would soon become known by a different name, a name that endures to this day: Armenia.

# Chapter 3 – A Conquered Armenia

Compared with other ancient powers, little is known about the race that captured Urartu in 585 BCE. The Medes were a mysterious group whose origins are shrouded in mystery. They had been living in the land of Media—part of modern-day Iran—for centuries, but they had been little more than a scattered group of tribes pretending to be a kingdom until Cyaxares became their first truly ambitious king and forged an empire out of them in 625 BCE. Within a few years, Cyaxares had captured the city of Nineveh, thereby conquering the Assyrians and making Media one of the most important powers of the ancient Middle East. By comparison, the weakened Urartu had been easy pickings.

Yet the glory day of the Medes would not last forever. No empire ever did, and Media would only continue unconquered for around 75 years before it, too, would meet its match in the form of another one of the greatest powers in antiquity: the first Persian Empire, also known as the Achaemenid Empire.

It is seldom that a conquering ruler, a man who built a vast empire and one who would go down in history with the epithet "the great," a man of war and incredible power, is remembered as being a merciful and benevolent king. Cyrus the Great was one of those men.

Legend has it that Cyrus was the crown prince of Media, but a prophetic dream caused his father, King Astyages, to throw him out into the wilderness when he was a baby. Cyrus was raised by lowly herders and returned to conquer the kingdom that was rightfully his, despite his humble upbringing. It is more likely that he was the son of a minor king in Astyages' realm and became the king of Persis in the early 6$^{th}$ century BCE. Either way, he might have borne the title of king, but he was a nobody—just another of Astyages' servants. That was the case until 550 BCE. Gathering a puny army, Cyrus set his sights on Ecbatana, the capital of Media and the seat of Astyages. Potentially with help from the Median commander—who was also sick of Astyages' rule—Cyrus conquered his overlord and became the most powerful man on the Iranian Plateau. He crowned himself king of Persia and was determined to build a far greater realm than Media had ever been.

And build a mighty realm he did. Cyrus would go on to defeat even the might of Babylon, then one of the greatest powers of the known world, without spilling a drop of blood. The people had heard of his benevolence and goodness to those he ruled over, and they threw the gates wide before him. Indeed, having overthrown the brutal oppressors who formerly ruled over Babylon, Cyrus was the one who set free the captive Jews, and in doing so, he probably saved the Jewish faith (and the following Christian one) from obscurity. He is also credited with composing the Cyrus Cylinder, the first known bill of human rights, which stipulated that his subjects be allowed to live peacefully and practice their own culture and religion under his rule.

Cyrus the Great did succeed in founding a great empire, known as the Achaemenid Empire. And given that he had annexed all of the Median lands, Urartu—by then becoming known as Armenia—fell under Cyrus' rule. The people that were left after war and economic failure had crippled the kingdom were briefly permitted to live in some form of peace. But by 530 BCE, Cyrus was dead, most likely falling in a fight with rebellious nomads on the borders of his kingdom. And the Achaemenid kings that followed would prove to be far less kind—and far more typical of powerful kings—than their predecessor.

Soon, the Armenians, which were by then a race impoverished by the destruction of war, found themselves being deeply oppressed by the people who now ruled them. The Achaemenids began to tax Armenia heavily, and they wanted something that Armenia had only the very best of: horses. Fast, tough, and strong, Armenian horses were coveted for the constant warfare of an expanding empire, and the Achaemenids wanted lots and lots of them. In fact, Armenia had to pay an annual tax of 20,000 strong colts to the Achaemenid Persians. For a country whose economy was based on the production of young horses, this was a devastating blow.

The once-vibrant culture that had flourished during the glory days of Urartu now found itself crushed under the suffocating weight of necessity. The people who had been so dedicated to art and metalwork were now simply trying to make ends meet. They lived in small villages on the mountainsides in underground dwellings, no longer building strong stone homes or bustling cities. In fact, they were reduced to becoming semi-nomadic; depending entirely on flocks of sheep and herds of cattle or horses that the Armenians kept, they were forced to follow the grazing patterns, moving from summer to winter pastures. Even the stately vineyards that had once fueled the oldest winery in existence had disappeared. Instead, fields of barley had to be planted to be eaten as a staple. What little was left over was brewed into simple beer instead of the ancient wines that the people had once enjoyed.

In strong contrast to their suffering subjects, the government officials of Armenia (now a satrapy, or province, of the Achaemenid Empire) lived in comfort, pomp, and splendor. They had large houses with plenty of room to store all of the delicacies that the Armenians had been able to indulge in before the fall of Urartu, which included wine, beef, and raisins. And with tens of thousands of horses being shipped off so that Armenia's conquerors could go off and subjugate other nations just like them, there was no way that the common Armenian could find a way back to financial stability.

To rub salt in the wound, the shining culture of Armenia was shattered to its very core; even its religion was changed. While there is little evidence to suggest forced conversion, somehow during the two hundred years of the Achaemenid occupation of Armenia, the ancient faith of the Armenians was stripped away. In its place, the Armenians began to practice the same religion as the rest of the empire: Zoroastrianism.

One of the oldest monotheistic religions in the world, the origins of Zoroastrianism are obscure. Some say that it emerged around 1500 BCE; others claim that it found its roots around the time of Cyrus the Great. Either way, its first practitioner was a former polytheistic prophet by the name of Zoroaster. He told his followers about a vision he had received of a single ruling god, an idea that was utterly alien in a region that was mostly worshiping gods of the sun and sea. His ideas spread as far as the Achaemenids conquered, and it became the major religion of most of the Middle East and Asia until it was supplanted by Islam after the Muslim conquest of Persia around 651 CE.

To the Armenians, Zoroastrianism was a completely foreign concept, an idea far removed from the gods that their grandparents had worshiped. Yet it wormed its way into their hearts and homes, stripping away the relics of what they had once believed, the code by which their lives had once been lived. Their old faith was thrown to the wayside, and eventually, the majority of Armenia believed as their conquerors did.

The conditions chafed at the bruised Armenian psyche: the suffering, the struggle, and the knowledge that the taxes that hurt them were equally hurting other countries. For almost two hundred years, Armenia continued to suffer, but rebellion was brewing in the fertile ground of discontent.

Ever since it fell into the hands of the Achaemenids, the Satrapy of Armenia was ruled over by a satrap, or governor. In the 4th century BCE, one of these satraps would rise up in defense of his people.

Potentially Armenian by blood, in contrast with most satraps who were of Achaemenid royalty, Orontes I probably earned his way to his title as satrap of Armenia by proving himself in battle, fighting on the behalf of King Artaxerxes II against rebels in Cyprus. When Artaxerxes tried to order Orontes to move to a different satrapy, however, Orontes rebelled against him.

Orontes was not the only satrap who wanted change. Datames, satrap of Cappadocia, and Ariobarzanes, satrap of Phrygia, had also been fighting for change since 372 BCE in what is now called the Great Satraps' Revolt. Soon finding the support of the Egyptian pharaoh, Nectanebo I (whose successors would also aid in the fight, as Egypt was often an enemy of the Achaemenid Empire), the disgruntled satraps started to push back against their oppressive superiors. Orontes joined the fight in 362 BCE, ten years after Datames had begun the revolt, and at first, things looked promising for the people who trusted in him as being a savior. But their trust was deeply misplaced. Thanks to Egyptian help, the satraps succeeded militarily in many ways against the Achaemenids. The might of the Persian Empire was unable to crush the rebellion on the battlefield. Instead, it would be lost to the slow cancer of treachery, eating its way through the very heart of the revolt.

Ariobarzanes was the first to fall. Even though he had been supported by the powerful king of Sparta for three years, he failed to gain the support of his own son, Mithridates, who betrayed him to Artaxerxes II. The king had Ariobarzanes crucified and killed in 363 BCE. The following year, Datames was likewise betrayed, this time by his son-in-law.

The final blow to end the revolt came shortly thereafter. Nobody betrayed Orontes; instead, the Armenian satrap betrayed his own people. He turned against the revolt that he had once supported, and the Great Satraps' Revolt ended in ignominy and defeat. Orontes, however, was richly rewarded for ending the revolt; he was given many of the lands that had formerly belonged to Datames, his former comrade, and was allowed to keep his title as satrap of Armenia. Orontes' descendants would hold on to the title, too, making him the founder of the Orontid dynasty of Armenian satraps and, later, kings.

Despite the failure of the revolt, it would not be long before Armenia was freed from the fist of the Achaemenids. But, at least for a brief time, this freedom would catapult them out of the frying pan and into the fire. The Achaemenids were about to be defeated—not by their own unhappy people but by a far greater power. A young but nonetheless battle-hardened warlord, charging from the lands of the east, against whose fearsome armies not even the Achaemenid Empire could hope to stand a chance.

* * * *

Alexander was recovering from an illness, was vastly outnumbered, and had lived fewer years than the experienced commanders of the Achaemenid armies had been fighting battles. But he still believed that Persia would soon be his.

Only 23 years old, Alexander had been ruling over Macedonia for three years since the assassination of his father, Philip II. To honor his dead father's memory, Alexander was determined to finish what Philip had started: the conquest of Persia. Even though this quest may have seemed foolhardy for a mere youth with little experience to back him, Alexander believed that the gods were with him. Legend told how he had solved the unsolvable by untying the Gordian Knot (or, more accurately, sliced it in half) and how thunderstorms had been a good omen before the battle. But it was more than just luck that would play into Alexander's impending success: it was military brilliance.

Persian King Darius III had not yet fully tasted the young Macedonian's true skill. With an army 100,000 strong, Darius believed that not only could he put Alexander's troops to flight, but he could also cut off their retreat and butcher the lot of them, putting a stop to Macedonian aspirations once and for all. He could not have been more wrong.

There were about 40,000 Armenians in Darius' army the day that he met with Alexander on the coastal plains near Issus. Alexander, on the other hand, commanded about 30,000 men, his troops decimated by malaria and months of fighting. Yet the fiery young king, mounted on his trusted old black charger Bucephalus, inspired a blazing hope in his men and commanded them adeptly. Using the harsh terrain to his advantage, Alexander fought in the foremost ranks of his soldiers, tricking the Persians' experienced mercenaries into going toward perceived gaps in his offense that put them right where he wanted him.

Within a few hours, the Achaemenid Empire had been put to flight. Darius III was captured, and the Achaemenid Empire was no more.

As for the Armenians, who fought for an empire that had been taxing them so harshly for so many years, many of their numbers died as they had lived: cut down, bruised, and crushed on behalf of the Achaemenid Empire.

# Chapter 4 – An Empire in its Own Right

The Armenian Empire at its apogee under Tigranes the Great, also known as Tigran
*www.armenica.org Uploaded to en.wikipedia by en:user:Nareklm, CC BY-SA 3.0
<http://creativecommons.org/licenses/by-sa/3.0/>, via Wikimedia Commons
https://commons.wikimedia.org/wiki/File:Maps_of_the_Armenian_Empire_of_Tigranes.gif*

---

The life of Alexander the Great was a shooting star, a blazing comet that shone as bright as it was brief. Conquering Persia was just the start of his military success. The Battle of Issus made the way clear for him to march into the heart of Persia, and from there, he took Egypt in 331 BCE, followed by parts of Iran, India, and Babylon (modern-day Iraq). Nothing and no one could stand against him. He was the king of the known world, and he had expanded the borders of his tiny realm farther than even his ambitious father could have imagined.

In fact, Alexander's impact may have been even greater if a twist of fate had not cut short the illustrious life of this young emperor. He had his sights set on defeating Carthage and even Rome. If he had conquered the Roman Empire, the face of history might have looked very different. However, Rome would rule for over a thousand more years, thanks to a bout of malaria that claimed Alexander's life in 323 BCE. He was only 32.

While Alexander had expanded the borders of his kingdom, he had not given much thought to what would happen to it after he died, and immediately, the vast empire was in desperate peril. Alexander's wife, Roxana, was pregnant, and in his jealous rage, Alexander had killed every other male with any claim to the throne. While a regent, Perdiccas, was appointed, he decided to divide up Alexander's empire among a bunch of satraps. This was a fatal mistake. The satraps soon fell to fighting, trying to gain independence for their satrapies or even to seize the Macedonian crown for themselves. As quickly as Alexander's giant empire had been won, it melted just as quickly into chaos.

* * * *

For Armenia, the entire rule of Alexander had been a time of uncertainty. Things in the Achaemenid Empire had been difficult, but at least they had been familiar. Besides that, Armenia was starting to prove itself as one of the Achaemenid Empire's most important satrapies.

Darius III, the man who had been ruling over the empire at the time of its fall, had been a satrap of Armenia himself before becoming king. Maybe things were beginning to look up.

Maybe they would be worse under Alexander.

Alexander, however, had far bigger fish to fry than Armenia. It appears as though he might not have ever officially occupied it; he even allowed Orontes II, the satrap at the time, to keep his title. When Alexander's empire crumbled, Orontes saw his chance. Unlike his namesake—and likely his ancestor—who had betrayed his own people in the Great Satraps' Revolt, Orontes II wanted to build a better Armenia. For the first time in centuries, Armenia had the opportunity to be free.

This time, Orontes was successful. With the Macedonians fighting over the scraps, he was able to establish Armenia as an independent kingdom, ushering in the Orontid dynasty. His descendants would no more be satraps; instead, they were kings of a country all its own.

For over a hundred years, the Orontids ruled over an independent Armenia, slowly putting back together a country ravished by centuries of occupation. They were able to restore Armenia to something of its former glory, with new cities springing up everywhere. No longer did all the Armenians have to live in underground dwellings with their flocks and herds.

The Orontid dynasty, however, would be relatively short-lived. A beast had risen from the ashes of Alexander's empire—and that beast was hungry.

* * * *

Alexander's death fragmented his empire, and one of the bigger chunks would someday become a Hellenistic empire itself, forged by a man named Seleucus.

Placed in charge of Babylon under Perdiccas' regency, Seleucus, a Greek, was one of the satraps who wanted more. He won independence for his country, naming it the Seleucid Kingdom. It did not take long for the kingdom to become an empire, encompassing parts of Parthia, Greece, and India. And despite a crippling civil war just a generation ago, which saw the Seleucid Empire lose many of its lands, by the late 2$^{nd}$ century BCE, a new ruler had risen up. One who was determined not only to restore the empire to its former glory but to expand it even further.

Antiochus III the Great was more than just a king in the eyes of his subjects. He was a deity. Having established a cult around himself and his consort, he made himself vitally important to the people, gaining their wholehearted support for his campaigns. He was able to win back many of the eastern lands that had been lost during the civil war between his father and uncle, as well as conquering Lebanon and Palestine. It didn't take long before he set his sights on gaining even more lands—and Armenia was among them.

In 200 BCE, Orontes IV was overthrown by the Seleucid Empire, making him the last of the Orontid kings. Much of Armenia was brought under Seleucid control, at least for a brief time, as Antiochus plowed over his latest conquest and headed toward Rome. It would have been wiser to leave the mighty Roman Empire alone, though. The Romans defeated him in battle in 190 BCE and reduced his empire to only a handful of countries, effectively ending the Seleucid Empire when Antiochus was killed in 187 BCE, although it did manage to hang on, albeit weakly, until 63 BCE.

During the brief Seleucid occupation, Armenia had been divided into two separate satraps: Lesser Armenia and Greater Armenia. It was ruled over by a father and son named Zariadres and Artaxias, both Seleucid satraps that Antiochus had appointed. When Artaxias heard of

Antiochus' defeat by the Romans, he knew that the Seleucid Empire had sung its swansong. It would soon crumble into nothing, and then it would be every man for himself. There was danger in the situation but also opportunity.

It was an opportunity that Artaxias would seize with both hands. Setting himself up as the king of Greater Armenia, Artaxias I started to move to secure power for his country. Largely supported by the people, who had enjoyed their freedom under the Orontids (to whom Artaxias and Zariadres may have been related), Artaxias expanded Greater Armenia's borders and established it as a country in its own right once more. He was able to unify its diverse and scattered peoples and became one of the most famed governors of Armenia since its ancient beginnings. Immortalized in legend and song, Artaxias took advantage of the fact that trade routes between Rome and India ran through the country. Armenia flourished, and by 176 BCE, Artaxias was able to build a whole new city for his capital. Known as Artaxata, it may have been designed by the legendary Carthaginian general, Hannibal Barca.

Artaxias I became the founder of one of Armenia's most glorious dynasties: the Artaxiad dynasty. For almost a hundred years, one Artaxiad king after the other governed the country well enough that it was able to stand its ground in an era of relentless expansion and conquest. Artaxias had made Armenia an ally of Rome, and the Romans were all too happy to have Armenia as a buffer between their empire and their great enemies, the Parthians. But even Artaxias was nothing compared to the greatest of the Artaxiad kings. In 95 BCE, this great warrior ruler would rise to the throne. And despite unpromising beginnings, Tigranes II would prove to be the mightiest king of them all.

* * * *

Tigranes had been a prisoner for more than half of his life.

He had been only twenty years old when the Parthians, an old enemy of both Rome and Armenia, had finally gained the upper hand in their repeated attempts to invade Armenia. Mithridates II, the king of Parthia, had seized some parts of the country, and the current king of Armenia—Artavasdes I—was forced to negotiate peace or risk losing his entire kingdom. Artavasdes and the Parthians came to an accord at last in 120 BCE, but it was one that would be devastating for Artavasdes. He was forced to give up the parts of Armenia that Mithridates had annexed, and he was also forced to give up his relative, Tigranes. Sources differ on whether Tigranes was his son, brother, or nephew, but either way, the young man was a free Armenian, an heir to the throne, and shared a blood bond with Artavasdes. But the king had no choice. He had to send Tigranes to Parthia to become their hostage.

For the next 25 years, Tigranes would be trapped in a Parthian fortress. It is likely that he lived in a fair amount of luxury during that time and that his needs were well provided for, but one can only imagine how his heart longed for the wide skies, soaring mountains, and wild highlands of his youth. Tigranes had walked the mountainsides of Armenia not only as a free citizen but also as its future king. Now he was nothing but a pawn in the Parthians' game, an incentive for the Armenian king to keep the peace with Parthia or risk the death of the crown prince.

But Tigranes used that quarter-century in captivity wisely. He gained the Parthians' trust and learned their ways, and when the king of Armenia, Tigranes I, died in 95 BCE, Parthia decided that having a tame little king on the Armenian throne would do nothing but advance their own interests. Mithridates made the decision: Tigranes would be going home, as long as he yielded even more of Armenia's lands to the Parthians.

Tigranes, appearing as meek as a lamb, readily agreed. He ceded seventy valleys to the Parthians and made his way back to the land that he loved, finally taking the throne that was rightfully his. He must have been aware that the Parthians believed he would do whatever they asked and remain an easily manipulated ally.

They could not have been more wrong.

Knowing that Armenia needed help from a strong ally, Tigranes was quick to find a suitable princess to marry and thus gain the favor of her powerful father. That princess was Cleopatra the Elder, a princess of Pontus, which was a small but powerful nation on the banks of the Black Sea in modern-day Turkey. Less than a year into his reign, the new king began to expand his realm. His first aim was to annex Lesser Armenia, thereby unifying the two countries once again; he succeeded in this by 94 BCE.

In 91 BCE, Mithridates II—the same king that had held Tigranes captive for 25 years—died. Parthia was left in utter chaos, and Tigranes saw his chance to break free at last from the Parthian shackles and build the empire of which he had been dreaming all those long and weary years in captivity. He attacked the Parthians on the eastern border, wiping them out of the seventy valleys and regaining them for Armenia. This left no doubt in the Parthians' minds that the young man they had held captive for so many years was not going to kowtow to them any longer. Tigranes was no client king: he was a conqueror, and he was going to show the world what he could do.

Starting his campaign in 88 BCE, Tigranes did exactly that. His army was slow-moving, armed with tremendous siege engines and heavy cavalry, but wherever it went, it left a trail of destruction behind. By 87 BCE, he had sacked Ecbatana, once the royal seat of Cyrus the Great. All of Media fell at his feet, and that was only the beginning. Nation after nation would follow, bowing in the face of the Armenians that their imperial rulers had once so heavily subjugated: Cappadocia, Gordyene, Syria, Cilicia, and finally, Phoenicia. The latter was part of the tiny remnant of the Seleucid Empire, which had sparked the Artaxiad dynasty in the first place. It was crushed now in the face of Tigranes' onslaught.

This great king was more than just a conqueror, however. He also saw to it that his economy flourished, which helped to fuel his constant thirst for expansion as well as helping his people to thrive. The trade routes that characterized the glory of the Artaxiad dynasty were reopened and strengthened. Good relations with Babylonia made for better trade, and Armenia was mined for its abundant natural resources, with minerals like iron and salt finding their way all over the known world.

For the Armenians, a nation that had known deep oppression, it was heady stuff to be on the side of a conquering warlord. While Tigranes II seems to have treated most of the conquered nations with a fair amount of grace by allowing their kings to remain on their thrones, albeit as his vassals, Armenia was at last on the winning side. The Armenian people got to see their king riding through the countryside on one of those fiery horses that had made Armenia famous in the ancient times; Tigranes always wore a glittering tiara studded with precious stones that flashed in the sunlight like the flanks of his plunging charger, and even better, he was followed by four men on foot. These were not servants—they were subjugated kings who acted as his advisers, but they were not given the privilege of riding a horse like Tigranes was. He was the self-proclaimed king of kings, and he made sure that his vassals knew it as they ran alongside his horse in the heat and dust.

Armenia was victorious—for now. Like Alexander the Great, who was once Armenia's conqueror, Tigranes' empire would be as short-lived as it was brilliant.

# Chapter 5 – Caught in the Crossfire

When Tigranes II married Cleopatra the Elder, the daughter of King Mithridates VI of Pontus, it had been a strategic move, just as the majority of royal marriages at the time were. At war with Rome, Pontus was a desperate nation, one that would be glad to ally itself even with a weakened country like Armenia. Yet becoming an ally of Pontus would prove to be Tigranes' greatest mistake.

At its height, the Armenian Empire encompassed parts of modern-day Israel, Turkey, and Iran, among others. It had fought victories against Parthia, Judea, Cilicia, and Syria, and it was ready to become an even greater kingdom. Yet one great power that Armenia had never faced in battle was Rome. The Roman Empire had been an Armenian ally for decades, even though Tigranes' rapid expansion had led to rising tensions between the two nations. Yet all that would change thanks to a bad decision Tigranes had made at the very beginning of his long and illustrious reign.

Cleopatra the Elder herself had proven to be a good enough wife for Tigranes. She wasn't the problem. However, if there was anything that Cleopatra had in abundance, it was daddy issues. Her father, Mithridates VI, was so instrumental in sparking three massive conflicts with Rome that they were named the Mithridatic Wars.

Mithridates was a particularly colorful character—and a particularly nasty king, but a glimpse into his past reveals that he had good reason to be. After his father was assassinated when Mithridates was just thirteen years old, his mother, Laodice VI, became the regent in his stead. Laodice, however, had plans to take her son's life in order to extend her own power. Mithridates fled into hiding for years before returning to cast his mother into prison and potentially assassinate his own brother, seizing power for himself. He had been fighting a war with Rome ever since.

By 75 BCE, the Third Mithridatic War was in full swing, and this time, Pontus was losing. Mithridates—by now a paranoid old man who took small doses of poison every day in a bid to build up an immunity against assassination—was forced to flee Pontus, running to the arms of his son-in-law, the mighty Tigranes the Great. Respecting the fact that Armenia had long been an ally, the Romans sent messengers to Tigranes, requesting him to surrender Mithridates to him. It would have been best for Tigranes if he had done so. Yet Mithridates, though by now useless as an ally, was still his father-in-law. Perhaps persuaded by his wife, Tigranes refused to let Mithridates go.

Furious, the Roman consulship declared war on Armenia, and Lucius Licinius Lucullus led a powerful Roman army to march on Tigranocerta, the new capital that Tigranes had ambitiously built and named after himself. Tigranes made his stand there on October 2$^{nd}$, 69 BCE, but it was a fruitless one. Lucullus' men put him to flight, and the

Armenian army that had recently been so successful in its conquests had no choice but to flee back toward the former capital of Artaxata. By September of the next year, Tigranes had been beaten again at Artaxata, and the winter that was rolling in over the Armenian mountaintops was one of the bleakest Tigranes had ever seen. A winter that maybe even left him nostalgic for a Parthian prison.

But by a stroke of luck, that was not the winter that Tigranes lost his empire. Lucullus' troops, plagued by disease and hesitant to suffer through another brutal Armenian winter, launched three separate mutinies over the next few months. Lucullus was recalled to Rome in 67 BCE, giving Mithridates and Tigranes both a chance to recover. Mithridates even managed to get some of his lands back, and Tigranes was able to defeat his rebellious son, Tigranes the Younger.

However, Tigranes the Younger knew that the fight with Rome was not over yet. With his tail between his legs after his father had soundly beaten his rebellion, the young man fled not to Lucullus, but to a Roman general who was rapidly engraving his name deep in the face of history: Pompey.

By 66 BCE, this statesman was already known as Pompey the Great and had enjoyed two glorious triumphs in Rome for his military achievements in Sicily and Africa. Where Lucullus failed, surely Pompey would succeed. He marched on Pontus and set Mithridates once again to flight, this time to hide in the depths of Crimea; then, Pompey turned toward Armenia. Tigranocerta was still largely destroyed, practically abandoned after Lucullus had sacked it in 68 BCE; Tigranes himself had clawed back Artaxata once Lucullus had gone and was hiding out there, and so, Pompey marched on the substitute capital, ready to raze it to the ground just like Tigranocerta.

But the loss of his former capital had broken the great Armenian king's heart. Tigranocerta had been his magnum opus, a magnificently

Hellenistic city that bustled with culture and commerce. Tigranes was old by now and tired and wealthy, and he had had enough of fighting. When Pompey reached the gates of Artaxata, Tigranes decided it would be better to give up his belongings in order to make peace. He surrendered to Pompey with hardly any fighting.

Tigranes was a beaten man, but Pompey treated him largely with respect. He was allowed to keep his throne in Armenia, provided that he was more or less a client king of the Roman Empire; however, he had to surrender most of his lands, keeping only Armenia itself alongside Sophene and Gordyene. Still, Tigranes was allowed to live out his days in peace, even though the Armenian Empire was no more.

Mithridates VI, however, was not so lucky. Paralyzed by fear of the Romans and devastated by his losses in the Mithridatic Wars, the Pontic king died a slow and terrible death. First poisoning all of his wives and children, he then swallowed a hefty dose of the toxin himself. Unfortunately, possibly due to having built up so much immunity against poison over the years, the poison failed to kill him immediately. He then tried to take his life by his own sword, but his weakened hand could not drive the blade fully home. He died slowly and in horrible anguish, finally meeting his demise when his own men butchered him out of mercy.

* * * *

Following the end of the Armenian Empire, Armenia became a Roman protectorate. This was a considerable advantage for Rome, which was still embroiled in conflict with Armenia's eastern neighbor, Parthia.

The same nation that had kept Tigranes the Great captive for so many years was still at war with Rome, and since Armenia now effectively belonged to the Romans, it was compelled to provide men and resources in order to fight the Parthians.

This first occurred in the early years of the reign of Tigranes' son, Artavasdes II. Tigranes had lived out the rest of his rule in peace, dying in 55 BCE around the age of 85, and had left the kingdom to Artavasdes.

Artavasdes was keen to prove to his Roman allies that he was a worthy successor of his famous father, so when war between Rome and Parthia broke out again in 53 BCE, he was quick to volunteer reinforcements to the Roman general, Marcus Licinius Crassus. But Crassus was reluctant to share the glory or spoils with some other king. He was the commander of the most elite army in the whole world, after all—there was no need for help from some barbarian king. Crassus could defeat the Parthians all by himself, and so, he rode off with his glittering regiments in their shining armor, rejecting Artavasdes' offer.

It was one of the last mistakes that Crassus would ever make. Lured into the open by the swift horseback archers of the Parthian army, he would quickly find out that his enemy was more than just a bunch of uneducated hooligans. Those sure-footed Iranian horses could spin and run with the kind of agility that the ponderous Roman legionnaires could not face. And in the summer of 53 BCE, the Roman invasion had turned into a rout. Crassus was killed, and the Romans fled with their tails between their legs, the Parthians in hot pursuit. They made it all the way into Armenia itself, where they forced Artavasdes to join their side, marrying the Parthian crown prince to Artavasdes' sister.

For the next fifteen years, the Parthians would be left alone, allowed to gloat over their fallen enemies in Rome as they exploited the resources of Armenia. Artavasdes II was discontent, but he knew better than to try and fight off a nation that had defeated the mighty Roman Empire itself. But Rome wasn't done with Parthia, and neither was one of its most accomplished generals, Marcus Antonius, better known to history by his Shakespearean name, Mark Antony.

In 36 BCE, Antony headed into Armenia, determined to fight back against the Parthians that had given Crassus such an ignominious defeat. A wiser general than his ill-fated predecessor, Antony not only accepted Artavasdes' help: he demanded it. Artavasdes was only too glad to switch sides. His entire country had suffered the same imprisonment in which his father, Tigranes the Great, had been condemned to endure for 25 years. Thanks to stronger Roman shields and the use of the tortoise formation to guard against those horse archers, the Parthians were chased out of Armenia and back into their own country.

Armenia was liberated from Parthian rule, yet as soon as Antony had left the country in order to march on Parthia itself, Artavasdes got cold feet. He remembered seeing the defeated legionnaires of Crassus stumbling back home through Armenia, their ranks shattered, their leader killed, and he did not have the stomach to send his own men off to suffer the same fate. When Antony's Parthian campaign ended in disaster, he blamed the fickle Armenian king for failing to provide enough reinforcements. So, Antony turned the remnants of his troops around and attacked Armenia, arresting Artavasdes for treason and carrying him back off to Alexandria—the home of Antony's famous mistress, Cleopatra.

There, Antony held a mock Roman triumph, an act which Rome itself considered a defilement of a true triumph. Bringing up the rear of the grand parade was Artavasdes II and his family, bound in golden chains, booed and jeered at by the exuberant crowd. Artavasdes would never be a free man again; he would be beheaded on Cleopatra's orders within a few years, and the Artaxiad dynasty, once the heyday of Armenia, would effectively die with him. Although the dynasty would linger on until 12 CE, it was very weak, with the kings often hiding from their enemies.

* * * *

After the death of Artavasdes II and the conquest of Armenia, the country would be reduced to a kind of plaything caught in a vicious tug-of-war between Rome and Parthia. First, a Roman-backed king would find his way to the throne, then a candidate supported by Parthia, and so on, back and forth for almost a century until finally a Parthian named Tiridates was nominated to become king in the early 1ˢᵗ century CE.

Of course, this sparked an immediate war with Rome, once again. Emperor Nero was not amused with having a Parthian in charge of the land that was once a useful buffer zone between the warring nations, and for several years, Armenia was once again torn limb from limb in conflicts between Rome and Parthia. The fighting only ended in 63 CE when an uneasy peace was reached at last: Parthia would nominate the Armenian king, but only a Roman emperor could actually crown him. Nero begrudgingly agreed, and Tiridates I had his coronation in Rome with suitable pomp. He became the founder of the Arsacid dynasty.

The treaty between Rome and Parthia, however, was not as lasting as Tiridates' dynasty. Vespasian, who became the Roman emperor in July 69 CE, was quick to annex Armenia entirely. Under Roman protection, Armenia was reduced to a province of the empire, but nonetheless, it had a brief period of peace at last.

After centuries of warfare, Parthia itself was also starting to decline in importance. By the reign of Hadrian in the early 2ⁿᵈ century, Parthia appears to have been tired of fighting with Rome, and Armenia became more trouble than it was worth for the great old empire. Hadrian gave the country its independence, and for the first time since Tigranes the Great, Armenia was free once again.

As usual, its freedom would be short-lived. Another power was rising up in the ancient world. And the Parthians were nothing compared to this new Persian force.

# Chapter 6 – Illumination

Lucius Verus was the emperor of Rome—a title that he found most troublesome.

Raised in the house of Antonius Pius, Lucius had had nothing but good role models to follow growing up: Antonius Pius was well known for being one of Rome's most astute emperors, while Lucius's adoptive brother, Marcus Aurelius, would go down in history as a philosopher emperor. Marcus was a Stoic, a man whose belief in moderation and simplicity was deep and steady. Lucius was anything but. It had been an annoying interlude in his life of opulence and constant partying when Antonius had died in 161 and left the Roman Empire in the hands of his two adopted sons, but Marcus had luckily taken up most of Lucius' slack, allowing him to do whatever he pleased.

That was until that pesky Parthian king, Vologases IV, marched on Armenia and set up one of his generals as its king. He had been waiting for Antonius to die, and it was less than a year since Marcus and Lucius had become emperors of Rome. Marcus knew he had to stay where he was and consolidate his power, so he sent Lucius to deal with the Parthian problem.

How irritating, Lucius thought. Never mind—perhaps there was fun to be had in the Middle East.

* * * *

Despite Lucius Verus' lackadaisical attitude, he had talented generals, and most of them were quite relieved that he elected to stay at his new resort in Syria instead of getting his hands dirty. Generals like Marcus Statius Priscus and Gaius Avidius Cassius were able to win yet another fight with Parthia over Armenia, reinstating the Arsacid dynasty in 166 CE. Lucius, who had never even seen Armenia, bestowed upon himself the title of Armeniacus to celebrate "his" victory.

It was the last time that a Parthian would sit on the Armenian throne. The Parthian Empire, which had been a thorn in Rome's side for five hundred years, was falling into decline. It had stood against the might of Rome for so many centuries, but the Romans would not be the ones to defeat it; instead, it was the Parthian nobility themselves that staged an uprising and overthrew their king. Ardashir I, a former king of Persis, killed the Parthian king, Artabanus IV, in 224. He claimed to be a descendant of Sasan, a legendary hero, and thus, the dynasty he founded was named the Sasanid dynasty. It would rule over Persia for over 400 years, and Ardashir was the first to call his country by the name it bears today: Iran. He also took the same title that Tigranes the Great of the Armenian Empire had born, *Shahanshah*, or "king of kings."

The fall of Parthia, an empire that had devastated Armenia for so many centuries, was only a brief respite for the Armenian people. They had not asked to be involved in half a millennium of conflict, caught as they were between the two great powers of the ancient world, and yet their suffering was not over. In 252, the Sasanids attacked. They feared that the Armenian Arsacid kings, who had blood ties through Vonones I to the old Parthian royalty, would make an attempt to claim the Persian throne. They invaded, and Rome retaliated. Once again, Armenia was reduced to a battlefield that was not respected by either one of the nations at war on those windswept highlands.

In the very same year that the Sasanids first invaded, Ardashir's son, Shapur, ordered one of his minions—a man known as Anak—to assassinate the royal family of Armenia. Anak butchered the queen, and the king, Khosrov II, was killed soon afterward. The only remaining male heir to the Armenian throne was a two-year-old boy named Tiridates. His relatives were quick to smuggle him to safety as his country was ripped apart without a king to lead it. Meanwhile, the remaining Armenian nobility captured and executed Anak and his whole family—except for a little boy named Gregory. And these two children, who had suffered such a deep and mutual tragedy, would change Armenian history forever.

* * * *

Tiridates had been raised in a Roman court. Despite the fact that Rome's argument with Armenia had caused the country so much grief over the centuries, Rome remained Armenia's key ally, and considering that the Persians had killed his family, Tiridates had nowhere else to turn. He was a helpless little toddler when he was brought to the great city, and he would remain there for the rest of his childhood.

But once he was a grown man, Tiridates knew that he could not hide in the safety of Rome forever. He had to go back to the country that he did not remember. The country that was his ancestral homeland.

The country that needed him to rise up as king.

When Roman Emperor Marcus Aurelius expelled the Sasanids from Armenia in 270, the twenty-year-old Tiridates saw his chance. He traveled back to Armenia, and the people rallied around him, helping him to keep back the relentless tide of Persian invaders. The Sasanid

Empire fell into a state of civil war, and Tiridates was able not only to strengthen his borders but also to win parts of Assyria for his army.

By 298 CE, Tiridates III had unified his entire country, and he had found a powerful and close ally in the emperor that had grown up in the city alongside him: Diocletian. Having murdered a usurper with his own hands, Diocletian had come to power in 284 CE and supported Tiridates in his conquests. They were united in a common thread of hatred. Tiridates, with only traumatic memories of his murdered family, hated the Sasanids. And Diocletian, strongly influenced by his right-hand man Galerius, hated the Christians. He would be made famous for being one of the harshest persecutors of Christianity in the history of the Roman Empire.

Tiridates, for his part, was different from most Armenians in that he did not practice Zoroastrianism with the same dedication as the rest of his people. The ancient religion had been part and parcel of Armenian culture for around eight hundred years, but it was still a Persian religion, and Tiridates hated it. Instead, he was a pagan, practicing the old polytheistic faith that had been in Armenia long before Zoroaster ever walked the earth. But there was a new player in the religious game of Armenia, too. Ever since the mid-1st century CE, when Thaddeus and Bartholomew—two of Jesus' original disciples—brought the Gospels to Armenia, the people had been practicing early Christianity. And despite the looming threat of persecution from Diocletian, Armenians held steadily to this new faith.

This faith had found footing in Cappadocia, too, where Christian schools had been flourishing. And in one of these schools, a little boy had grown up, a boy who bore the burden of a bloodstained family conscience on his shoulders. His name was Grigor Lusavorich, although he would go down in history as Gregory the Illuminator. And he felt profoundly guilty for the fact that his father, Anak, had murdered the

Armenian royal family.

Gregory had been improbably rescued after his whole family was executed and taken to Cappadocia, where he could have lived a quietly anonymous life if he had chosen. Instead, spurred on by his shame and a desire to right his father's wrongs, Gregory traveled to Armenia as a young man and was given a position in Tiridates' court at Vagharshapat as a palace functionary. Every day, he lived and worked in the very shadow of the man who had grown up a bitter orphan because of what his father had done. And every day, Gregory clung to the faith that was the only reason he could believe he was somehow forgiven. That he was somehow redeemed.

That faith had changed his life. And it would change Armenian history.

* * * *

Anahit was the pagan goddess of healing and fertility, and in Tiridates' eyes, she was the glory of his nation. Depicted as a beautiful young woman, Anahit had bronze and golden statues all over Armenia, and her cult had been flourishing for four hundred years. Tiridates worshiped her wholeheartedly, and his entire retinue was expected to do the same—including Gregory, the secret Christian.

It was likely a bright day in spring or summer, as it was the day of a religious ceremony dedicated to the golden goddess whose gleaming statue shone in the court of Eriza, where Tiridates had made his pilgrimage to pay his respects to the mother goddess. His retinue carried wreaths of flowers, ready to lay them down as sacrifices at the feet of Anahit. One by one, Tiridates' servants obediently did so until only one young man was left. Annoyed that he had not taken the initiative, Tiridates ordered him to lay down his wreath.

And Gregory did the unthinkable. He defied the king.

Taking a stand, the young servant refused to lay his garland of flowers at the golden feet of the statue of Anahit. He told the king and everyone watching that he did not practice polytheism the way they did—he was a Christian, and he would rather die than deny his faith.

The move was one of not only religious but also political significance. Tiridates had no choice but to deal harshly with this young man; no one, especially not some lowly servant, could be allowed to get away with defying the king of Armenia. Gregory was in trouble even before Tiridates found out that he was the last surviving member of Anak's family. Nothing could have pacified the king in his burst of royal rage. He ordered Gregory to be cast into Khor Virap, the "bottomless pit," a dark and terrifying underground dungeon from which no one returned alive. This likely occurred around 288 CE if the legend is accurate.

The legend of Gregory and Tiridates III grows murky with the years, and it is difficult to separate fact from fiction, but the story goes that Gregory languished in Khor Virap for thirteen terrible years. He only survived thanks to a kind old lady who used to bring him scraps of bread; Tiridates, meanwhile, ordered the Christians to be persecuted, a move that would soon be echoed by his friend Diocletian.

History is sure that Tiridates continued to expand Armenia, establishing it back into an echo of its former glory, a feat for which he would become known as Tiridates the Great. Diocletian was instrumental in assisting him. By 299, the Sasanids had been resoundingly defeated and cast out into their own country, and Armenia was no longer a mere province of the Roman Empire. Instead, it was a protectorate and had been granted more independence than it had enjoyed in a long time. Satisfied with his work, Diocletian returned to Rome to persecute Christianity in his own realm.

By that time, Gregory had been in the ghastly dungeon for eleven long years. He would languish there for two more years before a legendary disease began to afflict the king. Tiridates was struck with what was then known as lycanthropy; he began to behave "like a wild boar," stumbling around as if lost in the palace and its grounds, his mind leaving him. None of the pagan priests or Armenian physicians could do anything for him.

His relief would come from the unlikeliest quarter. Khosrovidukht, Tiridates' sister and fellow survivor of Anak's assassination, had a dream that Gregory was still alive and that he was the only one capable of curing Tiridates' affliction. It was a long shot, but she knew that she had to try. She retrieved a weak and sickly Gregory from the prison and brought him to Tiridates, and when he laid his hands on the raving and ailing king, the disease lifted from him miraculously. It was enough to cause Tiridates to convert on the spot. He became a Christian, and seeking a means with which to defy the Sasanids—who were still deeply faithful pagans and Zoroastrians—he made Armenia the first country to officially adopt Christianity as its state religion in 301.

For his actions, Gregory was canonized. He is known to history as Saint Gregory the Illuminator, the patron saint of Armenia.

# Chapter 7 – Immortals and War Elephants

**Illustration II: The Battle of Avarayr, as imagined by Eduard Isabekyan**

*Eduard Isabekyan (Uploaded by: Irina M. Isabekyan), CC BY-SA 4.0*
*<https://creativecommons.org/licenses/by-sa/4.0>, via Wikimedia Commons*
*https://commons.wikimedia.org/wiki/File:The_battle_of_Avarayr.jpg*

The fact that Tiridates III had become a Christian, a religion that was being heavily persecuted by Rome at the time, did not put a stop to religious persecution in Armenia. Sadly, instead of stopping the practice altogether, Tiridates simply switched sides. He was utterly determined to see Christianity become Armenia's dominant religion—and not simply for pious motives. Instead, Tiridates saw Christianity as an act of defiance against the hated Sasanids, and so, he also saw every person who failed to worship the way he did as a threat to his throne and a potential ally of Persia.

Pagans, those who practiced the same polytheism that Tiridates once so fervently had, were subject to the same brutal treatment that the Christian Armenians had suffered prior to 301 CE. Temples and statues were destroyed, and many historical texts by pagans were burned, leaving a great black hole in Armenian history thanks to the wrath of the king.

The ancient world was experiencing a seismic shift when it came to religion. The polytheism and Zoroastrianism that had dominated the world was living on borrowed time. Only a decade after Tiridates was baptized, the Roman emperor Constantine converted, too. His move of the empire's capital to Byzantium marked the beginning of a rift of ancient Rome, splitting the empire into two: the Western Roman Empire, with its capital in Rome, and the Byzantine or Eastern Roman Empire, with its capital eventually finding its way to Constantinople—modern-day Istanbul.

Despite strenuous resistance from the pagans, which eventually culminated in a pitched battle of pagan forces against the might of Tiridates' army and ended in inevitable victory for Tiridates, the king succeeded in turning Armenia into a predominantly Christian nation. Gregory, of course, was its first archbishop. Armenia had to find its way now in a world that was rapidly shifting and changing as antiquity began to blend quietly into the Middle Ages.

The everyday Armenian was no longer allowed to have idols in his home or pray to his ancestral gods. He could no longer mourn in the traditional ways, which often took place in the form of lamenting dances that involved actually cutting one's own skin. Nor could a man marry several wives; marriage, formerly a loose arrangement that had little to do with the law, became a more formal institution, recognizable to modern-day marriages. The old rituals were dead, and a new world was being ushered in, one that many Armenians found repugnant. However, particularly supported by Gregory, charitable institutions were also springing up around Armenia thanks to its Christianization. These included hospitals and orphanages, as well as special homes for lepers.

By the end of the 4th century, Armenia had become mostly Christian, with the final pockets of pagan resistance being weeded out. The Western Roman Empire had largely lost interest in the little nation, but the Byzantine Empire still faced the Sasanids across the bruised buffer zone formed by Armenia. Just like Rome and Parthia, the Byzantine Empire and the Sasanids played a bloody tug-of-war with Armenia, disregarding the lives of its innocent citizens. Despite Tiridates' fervent war on the Sasanids, by the end of the century, the Armenian kings were more or less client kings for the Sasanids. They were barely able to make any choices without Persian approval.

The start of the 5th century, however, ushered in a time of hope—a so-called Golden Age and the swansong of the Arsacid dynasty. This time was carried on the feet of Saint Mesrop Mashtots, a monk with a powerful vision to change the lives of the people of his country.

The original Holy Bible had been written predominantly in Hebrew and Greek. As Christianity spread wildly across the world, the Bible began to be translated so that more and more common people would be able to read it. Jerome of Rome was one of the first, translating the entire

Bible into Latin in the late 4ᵗʰ century; the Goths, a Germanic tribe, were hot on his heels and translated the Bible into their now-extinct language, Gothic. Armenia's rising Christian population was clamoring for a Bible of their own, one that even the common man could understand. Educated Armenians could all likely speak both Greek and Latin, but commoners spoke the various dialects of Armenian.

The only trouble with translating the Bible into Armenian was that it more or less failed to exist as a written language. Despite the fact that the language had been spoken for thousands of years—ever since Urartu—it had seldom been used for writing. Mesrop was determined to change that, as he wanted to spread the Gospels across the kingdom by making its holy text more accessible to all Armenians in their own tongue.

Mesrop had been born a Mamikonian. This noble Armenian family was rapidly proving itself to be almost as powerful as the Arsacids themselves; their members were educated and important in Armenian politics, being brought close to the king. Mesrop was no exception. A gifted linguist from the start, he worked alongside King Khosrov IV, writing laws or edicts for him. But Mesrop's heart was not in politics. He wanted to dedicate himself to a humbler life, one of piety and service, and so, he became a monk and joined a monastery around 395 when he was in his thirties. A few years earlier, Khosrov had been deposed by dissatisfied Sasanids. They made another member of the Arsacid family, Vramshapuh, king in his stead.

That is not to say that Mesrop faded from history. Far from it. Allying himself with Isaac the Great, the archbishop of Armenia, Mesrop expressed his determination to turn Armenian into a written language that the people could use to read the Scripture and worship. Despite the fact that this was a risky move for a king so deeply under the Sasanids' thumb, Vramshapuh agreed to lend his assistance, too, in the form of support and funding. By 405 CE, Mesrop had designed a 36-letter

Armenian alphabet uniquely suited to this ancient language. Together with Isaac and a Greek named Rufanos, Mesrop spent the next five years translating the first Armenian Bible, known as the Mesropic Bible.

The invention of the Armenian alphabet and the spread of the Bible in the native Armenian language marked the beginning of a Golden Age for Christian literature. Armenia had, at last, a voice in the realm of writing, and written works abounded in the language. It began to seem as though Armenia had a place in the world after all, despite continuous oppression from the Sasanids. But this rise in Armenian national identity did not sit well with their enemies in Persia. Armenians were starting to realize that they were unique, that they were their own people with their own religion and language, something very separate from the Sasanids. This pride and knowledge were dangerous, and it would have to be stopped. In just a few short years, the lives of everyday Armenians would change once again, as disaster was on the horizon.

* * * *

The Sasanid army came across the plain of Avarayr like something from Vardan Mamikonian's worst nightmares.

The commander of the Armenian people could trace his lineage back to St. Gregory, and he felt like he now knew an inkling of the fear that his ancestor had suffered in the depths of Khor Virap. And with good reason. Vardan was looking up at an army that had struck fear into the heart of Alexander the Great himself, an army that had become a legend for its fearsome qualities. He knew that even its appearance on the horizon was sending shivers down the spines of his largely inexperienced, disorganized band of rebels. Trying to keep up their spirits, he called back to them that God was with them. That whatever happened on this day, they would live or die for the Lord they served, on their own terms and not bowing to Sasanid demands.

It was just enough encouragement to keep the Armenian army rooted to the spot as they watched the heavy infantry marching toward them, their movements so synchronized that they appeared to be almost robotic. Their heavy shields were held in front of them, spears slicing the sky above them. The appearance of their infantry would have been intimidating enough, even if Vardan had not known that they were so indomitable as to be known as the Immortals. Wherever one of these infantrymen fell—and despite their light armor, they did not fall often—another would be ready to take his place. Fighting an Immortal was like fighting something you could not kill. He never seemed to be dead for long; there was always another, fresher, stronger one at the end of your blade once you had cut him down.

But the Immortals were only the half of it. Close on their heels, slow and lumbering under the weight of their enormous strength, came the war elephants. Murmurs of terror rippled through Vardan's ranks, and even he felt an insistent disquiet at the sight of these tremendous creatures. The foremost one paused, raised its trunk in the air as if to scent out the enemy. It threw open its ears, making it seem even bigger, and shook its head. The long white tusks caught the sunlight, and Vardan remembered all that he had learned about the war elephants that Persia brought from India. The towers on their backs were filled with armed men, but that was not what made the elephants dangerous. They were not simply beasts of burden. They were weapons in their own right; trained to trample and impale their enemies, they could crush a troop of cavalry, swiping a horse aside with a single blow of their tusks as if it was little more than a fly.

And Vardan Mamikonian was still standing his ground on the plain of Avarayr on this once-quiet morning of June 2$^{nd}$, 451, the stillness of the day shattered now by the sound of the marching Immortals and the trumpeting of the war elephants, even though he only had 66,000 men at his command. Even though he knew that this was fruitless, as they were facing the mighty Sasanids with what amounted to little more than a bunch of hopeful revolutionaries. There were some experienced Armenian fighters in his army, but Vardan knew that the bulk of his men were made up of ordinary people. Ordinary people who wanted to defend their way of life and their right to worship the God they loved. Their only hope was for the Byzantine reinforcements that Vardan had begged for to arrive in time—if they arrived at all.

It had all started in 428 CE. Having deposed a series of unsatisfactory kings, the Sasanids were growing testy with the Arsacid dynasty. The growing rise of Christianity was also perceived as exactly what Tiridates had wanted it to be: a threat to Persian authority. The Armenians were beginning to believe in a power even bigger than the Persians, and unlike Zoroastrianism, this power could not be wielded by Persian hands. It gave them hope, and hope was dangerous to the Persian king, Bahram V, for whom Armenia was a vital foothold in the continual war with the Byzantine Empire.

Bahram was not the only one who was concerned with the increasingly strong sense of identity pervading the Armenian psyche. The Persian nobility involved in governing Armenia was beginning to worry, too, enjoying their cushy lives under Sasanid protection while hating this new faith. They petitioned Bahram to depose the last Arsacid king, Artaxias IV, which he did in 428. Armenia was now little more than a Persian province.

For the Armenian nobility, including Vardan and his friends, this was no great trouble. Armenia had been ruled by Persia for decades, after all—the Persians protected them and did not oppress them too harshly. Artaxias had been little more than a figurehead anyways. But all that would change after Bahram died.

Bahram's successor, Yazdegerd II, was not the ruler that Bahram had been. Instead, he was determined to subjugate Armenia, not only physically but also spiritually. Yazdegerd could not care less what god the Armenians worshiped, as long as it was not their own god, one that was unique to them. One that gave them that dangerous identity. He petitioned them to join the Church of the East, from which the Armenians had seceded long ago, or better yet, to convert to the same religion that he followed himself, Zoroastrianism. But the Armenians held firm, and Yazdegerd grew tired of asking nicely. He sent his Zoroastrian priests into Armenia, backed by the military, and ordered them to destroy the Christian churches and build Zoroastrian temples instead.

The Armenian Christians found themselves being oppressed and persecuted once more, as the religion in which they found their identity was stripped cruelly away. Vardan Mamikonian was chief among those who were angered by this turn of events. He had once sympathized with the Persians, but those days were over now. He would lead his people to the religious freedom they deserved—or die trying.

Sadly, history would prove to favor the latter. Vardan's 66,000-strong band of fighters did not stand a chance against the Sasanids, of whom there were more than 300,000, with some of them being Armenians who favored Persian rule. The battle was brief, bloody, and decisive. Vardan and his men were butchered on that plain, and the elephants trampled their blood into the dirt.

\* \* \* \*

The Battle of Avarayr was a devastating defeat for Christian Armenia. However, even with Vardan dead, the Mamikonians still refused to give up. Vardan's nephew, Vahan Mamikonian, continued to fight against the Sasanids. This time avoiding a pitched battle, Vahan fought a long and grueling guerrilla war that nonetheless succeeded in wearing down

Sasanid resolve to impose Zoroastrianism. In 484 CE, the Nvarsak Treaty finally realized the late Vardan's vision: to allow Armenians to practice whatever religion they chose.

For his part, Vardan was made St. Vardan, and he remains a cultural hero to Armenians to this day. One cannot help but wonder how things would have turned out differently at the Battle of Avarayr if the Byzantine reinforcements had arrived the way the Byzantine emperor, Marcian, had promised. But relations between Armenia and the Byzantine Empire were far from over. An emperor with Armenian blood in his veins was going to take the throne, and he was going to be an Armenian hero in a new and even more gruesome war, a war that would last to the modern day.

# Chapter 8 – An Armenian Emperor

Despite the fact that Armenia had been little more than a disposable battleground to the Byzantine Empire for centuries, the tide was changing. Armenia would not be a mere pawn to Byzantium forever, not the way that it had always been to Rome. Armenian influence would grow in the Byzantine Empire, and it would change the importance of this bruised and bloodied country in history.

A new age was dawning. The ancient time was fading into the shadows; the years governed by Persia and Media, by Rome and Macedonia, were almost over. Yet the time of conquering warlords was nowhere near its end, and as the world began to shift into the Middle Ages, two mighty powers would emerge from the chaos. Powers that clash to this very day—and powers that would never clash harder than in Armenia.

But all that was centuries in the future. For now, Armenia's influence in the Byzantine Empire was growing. At first, Armenia had been to the Byzantines and Sasanids just what it had been to the Romans and Parthians, divided up twice in the late 4$^{th}$ and early 5$^{th}$ centuries as if it was little more than a cake and its people were mere decorations. Things had been made worse in 451 when Byzantine relief failed to save the Christian Armenians at Avarayr. Instead, while the Armenians were suffering their terrible defeat, the Byzantines were holding the Council of Chalcedon. The failure of the Armenian Church to be at the council resulted in a rift that divided the Eastern Orthodox Church from the Armenian Church, a rift that still exists to this day.

Yet even though the Byzantines treated the Armenians as being theologically inferior, they certainly had use of them in their armies. By the end of the 5$^{th}$ century, the Armenians from the Byzantine-controlled (and smaller) portion of Armenia made up the bulk of the army, and they had made such a name for themselves that the palace guards were handpicked from among their ranks. Eager to seek the prosperity that the Byzantine Empire offered, Armenians flocked to its nearby capital, which was then Byzantium. It has been said that the Armenian effect on Byzantine history has been vastly underestimated as Armenian military leaders worked their way up to fame and success in Byzantium.

Entering the 6$^{th}$ century, Armenia was still divided. The largest portion of its historical territory still belonged to the Sasanids, but in 582, all that was about to change.

Ever since the year 562, Byzantium and Persia had arrived at a forced treaty. Both were struggling with other invaders, and both knew that they could no longer afford to challenge one another and protect their own borders. An uneasy peace began, but Armenians in the Sasanid part of the country were unhappy with these arrangements. Byzantine Armenia was far more prosperous than Sasanid Armenia; added to that, while the

Sasanid Armenians were more or less free to practice Christianity, the Sasanids were still Zoroastrians. If the Armenians had to have overlords, they wanted them to be Christians. In 571, the peace was broken when Armenia revolted, and Emperor Justin II of the Byzantine Empire sent an army to fight the Sasanids on the Armenians' behalf.

It was a thrilling day for the Armenians when the Persian governor was driven out of his home at Dvin, an almost poetic victory in the light of the defeat at Avarayr more than 150 years earlier; their commander was named Vardan II Mamikonian, and he achieved what his namesake could not. But while the Armenians were doing well, the Byzantines fared poorly. The important city of Dara fell to the Persians in 573, a blow that utterly shattered Emperor Justin II. He suffered a mental breakdown and abdicated a year later, leaving the Byzantine throne to his general, Tiberius. The old general ruled for a further four years after Justin's death in 578 as Tiberius II Constantine, and upon his death, the Byzantine-Persian war was still raging. He knew on his deathbed that he would have to hand over the war to a young man who had proven himself in battle against the Persians, and that man was Mauricius Flavius Tiberius, who was crowned Emperor Maurice.

Maurice had witnessed firsthand the devastation that Persia had wrought in Armenia, as well as the abundant natural and human resources in the country. One of his first moves as emperor, after he was crowned in 582, was to renew the war on Persia. The bitter and bloody fight would continue until 591, and it was not the Byzantines' prowess that saved Armenia. Once again, it was trouble within Persia itself. Civil war broke out there in 589, and one of the opposing kings fighting to claim the throne, Khosrow II, sought Maurice's aid. In exchange for putting Khosrow on the throne, Maurice won back Armenia for Byzantium. This was a victory for the Armenians, but it was even more so a boon for Byzantium, as now there were even more Armenians available to fill up the ranks of the army with seasoned fighters.

Saving Armenia was not Maurice's only accomplishment as emperor. Over the next twenty years of his reign, Maurice succeeded in scraping back together a fragmented and shattered empire that was on the brink of collapse. His leadership shaped the Byzantine Empire into a force that would be able to withstand the breaking waves of time, far outlasting its western cousin. But for all the good that he had done, Maurice would die gruesomely. He had never treated his soldiers particularly well, spending his money frugally on them while focusing on other areas in his empire, and in 602, they revolted against him led by a man named Phocas.

Phocas was a centurion in Maurice's army, and he was a fairly good military commander—as well as a rather brutal human being. He succeeded in rallying the army to overthrow Maurice and claimed the title of emperor for himself, becoming one of history's most legendary usurpers and tyrants. Maurice did not have to live long with the humiliation of being defeated by a mere army officer, as he and his six sons were slaughtered by Phocas in 602.

For the next eight years, Phocas' rule would rain terror upon the subjects of the Byzantine Empire, and the Armenians were no exception. A zealous persecutor of Christianity, Phocas made the lives of most of his subjects fairly miserable. Armenia found itself fighting to defend the Byzantine border from a vengeful Khosrow, who was determined to overthrow the man who had usurped his ally, and in the war that followed, it was the Armenians who would be cut down by the thousands as the Sasanids once again trampled bloodily over their country.

Discontent spread wildly across the whole of the empire. Riots erupted in Byzantium as even the nobles started to rebel against Phocas, who had become nothing short of a tyrant. And in Armenia, there was little hope. They had been badly treated by the Sasanids, so they had looked for salvation from Byzantium, but now the Byzantines were treating them just as badly.

There was no Maurice coming to save them this time. But there was someone with Armenian blood in his veins. Someone determined to save his ethnic homeland and the whole of the ailing empire.

That hero was Heraclius. The son of an Armenian governor, although he had grown up in Carthage as a Greek, Heraclius was well aware that the blood in his veins originated on the highlands of Armenia. It was his Armenian father, aware of the plight of all the Byzantines, that first stirred up his heart against Phocas. And in 610, eight years after Phocas usurped the throne, Heraclius and his fleet sailed forth to Byzantium. Their plan was to lay siege to the capital in a large-scale revolt, but it was hardly necessary. By then, there was scarcely a man left in Byzantium who would fight on Phocas' behalf. According to some sources, by the time Heraclius reached the city walls, Phocas had been butchered by his own nobles. His corpse—robbed of the arms, legs, and head—was handed over to Heraclius as a gruesome trophy, and his head was carried around the streets of the city he had terrorized on a spear.

It is difficult to comprehend a more picture-perfect hero to the Christian population of the empire than Heraclius. A sturdy man in his thirties, Heraclius even looked the part; tall and powerfully built, he was a picture of magnificence in his gleaming armor, topped with a mop of hair so deeply golden that it might as well have been spun from the sunshine. With Maurice and his heir dead, he was considered the savior of Byzantium, the driving force that had spurred the nobles to revolt at last. He was promptly crowned emperor and was promptly faced with the Persian problem.

Phocas had made little attempt to stand against the Sasanids, who had wrought destruction and heartache on the empire, starting in the Holy

Land that was so precious to the hearts of a majorly Christian populace. The Sasanids overwhelmed cities as integral to the faith as Damascus and Jerusalem, and most abominable of all—in the Christian Armenians' eyes—they carried off the True Cross from Jerusalem. Of course, they had also reclaimed Armenia and continued their persecution of its citizens. The Armenians were besieged on every side, both physically and spiritually.

Heraclius' first priority was to end the war that Maurice had worked so hard to stop. He rode out against the Sasanids, and at first, he experienced one of the worst times of hardship that Byzantium ever suffered. Constantinople was besieged, and Egypt was lost, sparking famine throughout the empire as it was cut off from its major supply of grain. Despite losing the faith of his people as a result of his failures (and marrying his cousin, Martina), Heraclius managed to rally. In 622, he attacked the Persians in Armenia, and this time, they would be driven out for good. Heraclius, for all his other failings, did succeed in saving his homeland from the Sasanids. And it would be the last time that those Sasanids would ever occupy it.

Persia had been terrorizing Armenia ever since the days of Parthia. But a new power was about to rise up—a power that would overwhelm the Sasanids and, ultimately, prove to be the greatest threat of all to the Armenian people.

# Chapter 9 – Crusader State

The ruins of Ani
*Martin Lopatka, CC BY-SA 2.0 <https://creativecommons.org/licenses/by-sa/2.0>, via Wikimedia Commons https://commons.wikimedia.org/wiki/File:Church_ruins_in_Ani.jpg*

By the time Heraclius had finished his work, he had become unpopular among his own people for the tribulations that his war on Persia had put them through, but at least the Byzantines had been victorious. The

Sasanids, whose empire was in decline, had been forced back into Persia, and peace was reached at last.

Meanwhile, all the way in Arabia, a tremendous shift was about to change the course of history, creating ripples that are still powerfully felt today. Islam was on the rise.

Before the 7th century, Islam, as we know it, did not exist. It was only in the year 610 CE —the same year that Heraclius was defeating Phocas in Byzantium—that the Prophet Muhammad of Arabia, according to Islamic tradition, received visions from the angel Gabriel. Gabriel gave him a series of commands, inspiring Muhammad to begin preaching what he called the "true religion" around 613. His following grew with tremendous speed. Muhammad's ideas were not all alien; in fact, the new religion he was preaching shared many concepts and even respected prophets prevalent in Christianity and Judaism. They were readily accepted by many of his fellow Arabians, and by the time of Muhammad's death in 632, Islam was more than just the following of a single prophet. It was a religion in its own right.

As it is today, the majority of the original Muslims were ordinary peace-loving people who wanted what everyone in the history of the world has wanted: food, family, peace, purpose, and an understanding of the world around them. They wanted something to believe in. But sadly, even then, a group of radicals began to commit violence in the name of Islam. The first holy war had begun.

Muhammad's body was hardly cold when his followers, whom by now had established the Arab Caliphate, began to seek to extend their lands. While Muhammad had sent letters to the rulers of various powers—including Byzantium and Persia—his successors favored a more direct approach, one that would give them more wealth and glory. By 642, ten years after Muhammad's death, the caliph of the time, Umar, had set his sights on Sasanid Persia. The power that had stood up to

Byzantium for four hundred years was weakened now, and it did not stand a chance against the strong hordes of the Arabs.

With the Sasanids gone, the Arab armies were able to turn on their neighbors, the Armenians. For the first time in history, Armenia—now almost entirely Christian—was facing an Islamic foe. And it would not be the last.

* * * *

As the Arsacid dynasty had fallen, the city of Dvin had risen again. The capital of Armenia since the first Persian *marzpan*, or overlord, had taken hold of the city, Dvin was ideally situated for commerce and agriculture. Its stern walls were surrounded by luxurious green fields and the richest pasture that the country could offer. Those pastures had once been covered in the glittering shapes of grazing horses. The earth had once rung with the thunder of their hooves as the fleet-footed youngsters chased one another back and forth across the grass, biting and bucking and playing, just like their ancestors had done thousands of years ago when their athleticism first made Armenia famous. Men and women had fed, groomed, ridden those horses across the wide-flung grasslands and on the craggy mountaintops just about forty miles away from Mount Ararat. But now, the fields were trampled, the grass crushed underneath the feet of camels. The walls had been torn down, and the horses and the men that had loved them lay butchered in the very streets.

Sources differ slightly on how exactly it came about that the Arabs defeated Armenia, but it is known that there was defeat and that it was absolutely devastating. Even when Rome and Parthia, or Byzantium and Persia, had squabbled back and forth across the country, it had been because Armenia was valuable to them. They may have seen the people as mere cattle to fill the ranks of their armies, but at least they were useful cattle. The Armenians had seen so much war, but according to a contemporary Armenian historian named Bishop Sebeos, they had never seen anything like the Muslims.

Ever since the beginning of the Muslim conquest of Persia—around 639—the Arabs had been raiding the borders of Armenia, taking little chunks out of the country but were never quite successful. But with the Persians subjugated by 642, they could turn their full attention on Armenia. And even the seasoned Armenian armies, backed up by Byzantines when Heraclius' grandson, Constans II, was able to spare a few men, would soon find out that they were no match for the blazing wrath of the Arab armies.

Sebeos was an eyewitness to the terrible fate of Dvin. The city was not merely besieged; it was ransacked. According to this Armenian historian, the Arabs attacked it "with fire and sword," killing and capturing all that lived and burning everything else. By the time the Arabs were done with it, Dvin was no longer the bustling capital of the Armenia that Heraclius had rescued. With 12,000 people dead and 35,000 more (mostly women and children) taken captive, Dvin was utterly destroyed.

* * * *

The sad fate of Dvin was not the end of Armenia's troubles with the Arab Caliphate. After sacking Dvin, the Arabs pulled back for a while, returning in 643 with an even more devastating attack; this time, the Armenian governor, Theodore Rshtuni, managed to push them back. Eventually, however, Rshtuni submitted to Arabic rule. For the next several decades, Armenia was passed back and forth between the Arabs and the Byzantines. Anytime that Armenia submitted to the Arabs, it was attacked by the Byzantines; when it swore allegiance to the Byzantines again in 656, the Arab caliph murdered almost two thousand Armenian hostages. Armenia was once again between a rock and a hard place.

The rest of the 7th and 8th centuries were spent more or less under Arab rule. When Arabs attempted to impose Islam on the general population, rebellions were sparked, but none of them ever gained enough ground to fully throw off their shackles. Like Vardan Mamikonian on the battlefield of Avarayr, thousands of Armenians perished defending their right to worship as they pleased. Nonetheless, the Arabs soon realized that it was impossible to force the entire populace to convert to Islam. Despite the fact that Armenia had not been independent for centuries, its people still had a ferocious independence when it came to their beliefs, and they would not be dictated to when it came to that.

By the end of the $9^{th}$ century, a noble family of Armenians had risen from the general chaos of the country as being the most powerful: the Bagratunis. A shift of power, with the Khazars (a powerful group of Turkic nomads living in modern-day Russia) allying themselves with Byzantium, had left the Arab Caliphate far more cautious than in its early days. Armenia was once again providing a buffer between two warring powers—the Christian Byzantine Empire and the Muslim Arab Caliphate—and with their borders and armies run ragged by warfare, both were content to allow Armenia to become a no man's land. For the first time since the days of the ancient Romans, Armenia became an independent kingdom in 885.

The architect of this new independence was Ashot I. Already in his sixties by the time he actually became king, Ashot had been fighting for his country ever since he was a young man—and not only with the sword. An adept diplomat, it was Ashot who managed to convince both the Byzantines and the Arabs that an independent Armenia would only be useful to both of them. This was confirmed in 885 when each of the two clashing empires sent messengers to Ashot bearing a crown. So, with two crowns and a skilled wit, Ashot became the first king of the Bagratid Kingdom of Armenia.

And for 160 years, Armenia would flourish once again as a free country. Its rulers were wise enough, on the whole, not to pursue unnecessary conflicts with other countries, even as the major powers of the time were clashing violently with one another, and so, Armenia gained a reputation for being as peace-loving as it was diverse. Its population included both Muslims and Christians, and at the height of the Bagratid Kingdom's power, its capital city, Ani, became known as the "city of a thousand and one churches." A bustling center of culture, arts, and commerce, Ani was a jewel of the Middle Ages, a rare cultural gem to be found on the highlands of one of the oldest countries of them all.

But the glory days of Ani and of the Bagratid Kingdom of Armenia would be even more numbered than those of Urartu or the glorious kingdom over which Tigranes had reigned. A new power—also Muslim but not Arabic, this time—was growing in the region: the Seljuk Turks. Originating in modern-day Kazakhstan, the Seljuks were a warlike band of Muslim Turks bent on conquering their world, and they were supported by their fellow Muslims, the Arabs. First emerging in the early 11th century, the Seljuks conquered Persia and Iraq. Armenia was the logical next step.

Yet it was not the Seljuks who eventually tolled the death bell for this ancient kingdom. Instead, it was their former allies, the Byzantines, who ended the Bagratuni Dynasty and captured Armenia in 1045.

The day of the Seljuks was coming, however. The Byzantines would only hold on to Armenia for nineteen years before the Seljuk Turks attacked in 1064. Ani, once one of the busiest and most beautiful metropolises on the face of the Caucasus, the beloved center of Armenian culture and home to more than a hundred thousand people, fell to the Turks that same year. For the first time, Armenia was in the grip of the Turkish people, and that grip would last for many devastating centuries.

\* \* \* \*

Still, the Armenian people refused to let go of their Christian faith. And luckily for some of them, there were many Europeans who also felt compelled to cling to it—and to defend it, regardless of the cost in human life. These men were the Crusaders.

As a ferocious war erupted across the whole world, pitting Christian forces against the Muslims, many Armenians fled their own homeland. An exodus of Armenians streamed into nearby Cilicia, where the long arm of the Seljuks had not yet reached. There, the Rubenid dynasty founded the Armenian Principality of Cilicia in circa 1080. They might have been far from their ancestral homes, but the people were still Armenians, and here they were free to practice their culture and faith in relative peace.

Soon, these Armenians attracted the attention of another key player in this part of history: Pope Urban II.

The Byzantine emperor during the 1090s, Alexios I, had been begging the pope for help against a common enemy of the Christian world. Inspired by the prestige that he would gain if he managed to summon a combined army of Christian forces in a Europe that was being torn apart by petty wars among small kings, Urban was more than happy to help, calling an army together to attack the Holy Land, which was then under the control of those same Seljuks who had captured Armenia. The First Crusade was launched in 1095, and thousands of European troops traveled from as far away as Great Britain, France, and Germany and headed toward the utterly alien lands of the Middle East. And this is where the Armenian Principality of Cilicia caught their attention. In a world almost entirely dominated by Turks and Arabs, the Armenians might have been robbed of their homeland, but they had two things that the Crusaders needed: the Christian faith and fast horses.

The Armenians had brought some of their famous horses with them from their home, and when the Crusaders came to Cilicia asking for help, they were more than ready to assist them in conquering their mutual enemies. This small principality—arguably the first important Armenian diaspora community—became instrumental in the early successes of the First Crusade.

Sadly, however, the Armenian Principality of Cilicia would not be the last diaspora community that was forced to leave their home and thrive in a different world. A dark time was coming for Armenia. And considering all that the country's people had already suffered, it is significant that what was coming later would be the darkest time of them all.

# Chapter 10 – Conquered

As Greater Armenia continued to suffer under the subjugation of the Seljuk Turks, the Armenian Principality of Cilicia—brief though its heyday was—flourished all the more as Crusaders continued to stream through on their quest to liberate the Holy Land. In fact, the little principality was growing in such importance that it was about to become a kingdom, led by a man named Levon of the Rubenid dynasty.

Levon II (also known as Leo) was born a prince of Cilicia. Growing up, he was the heir apparent, the younger brother to its childless lord, Roupen (or Ruben) III. Politics were strained and difficult. The Byzantine Empire, in a stunning twist of affairs, had allied itself with one of the most legendary Muslim leaders of the Middle Ages—Saladin. This move enraged the Holy Roman Empire, which had grown from the wreckage of ancient Rome and was an avid participant in the Crusades, as they were closely linked with the papacy. Its leader was Frederick Barbarossa, a red-bearded larger-than-life legend of a man who would fight anyone, especially if they happened to be a Muslim. When Saladin took Jerusalem in 1187, enjoying his lack of opposition from Byzantine forces elsewhere, it was all the reason that Barbarossa needed to launch the Third Crusade.

As usual, Cilicia was instrumental in the Crusade, this time more than ever. The principality had grown in size and importance, thanks to Levon's adept management. His brother Roupen had been betrayed and imprisoned by a former ally, and he was so shaken by the experience that when Levon had come to his rescue, he handed over the ruling of his principality to his younger brother in 1187. It was only two years later, thanks to his alliance with Holy Roman Emperor Henry VI (who succeeded Barbarossa, who drowned while recklessly trying to cross a river in the Third Crusade) and Pope Constantine III, that Levon became a king and the Armenian Principality of Cilicia was raised to the status of the Kingdom of Armenian Cilicia in 1198. The Byzantine emperor had also attempted to make Levon king, but the two kingdoms were never able to settle their theological differences, and so, the Holy Roman Empire and the papacy beat the Byzantines to it.

During Levon's reign, the Kingdom of Armenian Cilicia reached its very apogee. His rule, ending in his death in 1219, was an era of hope and glory for a desperate people. It became larger than ever before, occupying much of what is now southern Turkey. While the Armenians back in their own homeland were being oppressed by the Seljuks, their culture was free to flourish, and their church to gain importance, in Cilicia. It was a foothold for the Armenian people, one without which their culture—and the Crusades —might have turned out very differently.

The fate of Armenia itself, however, would be very different during the Middle Ages. One Muslim power after another—each controlled by legendary military leaders whose skill and brutality made them as famous in their time as they are in ours—would overrun this unhappy kingdom. There was a brief respite during the 12th and 13th centuries as the Kingdom of Georgia rose up to overthrow the Seljuk Turks and take back Armenia for Christianity, but it was nothing more than a breather between blows. An even more legendary warrior than Saladin was about to march on Armenia, one whose impact on humankind was devastating: Genghis Khan.

* * * *

To the people of Europe and the Middle East, the world was smartly divided along one strong line: Muslims on one side, Christians on the other. There were wars within those powers, of course, but religiously and racially, there was a sense of "us" and "them," an undeniable divide that characterized the Middle Ages. Over the six hundred years since Muhammad had walked the earth, the Muslims had become a familiar, if intimidating, foe. They had effectively wiped Zoroastrianism off the face of the earth, and polytheism was a thing of the past for the most part, with paganism being buried alongside the old Greek and Roman gods. At least, so the people thought. Genghis Khan, like some ancient monster long buried in a black abyss, rose from out of nowhere to wreak havoc of a very ancient flavor on everything he touched.

Genghis Khan was born as Temüjin, and even his conception occurred under dark and frightening circumstances. His mother had just gotten married to a young man she probably loved when Temüjin's father, Yesükhei, kidnapped her on her way home from her wedding. He forced her into a marriage with him, and Temüjin was the product of their union.

By the time he was only sixteen years old, Temüjin's father had been poisoned, and Temüjin himself had been imprisoned for five years after murdering his older brother. It is not hard to see where the brutality of Genghis Khan came from. But with that brutality also came military and diplomatic brilliance. By the age of 27, Temüjin was made khan, or leader, of the Mongols; by 42, he had unified the scattered tribes of the region into the single powerful entity of Mongolia. And ten years after that, he devastated China, a land of around fifty million citizens, with an army only 100,000 strong.

Genghis Khan swept across the world before him like a tsunami: brutal, unstoppable, destroying all in its path. His soldiers were dark-haired, dark-eyed horsemen from a different world than the Middle Eastern people that he attacked once most of Central Asia was within his far-reaching grasp. It was not long before he turned to Armenia. To him, it was nothing, just a little kingdom, one more small jewel in his treasury. But to the people his forces would butcher, it was home.

Armenia, at the time, was a divided kingdom, split up between the powers that continued to war over it. Northern and Eastern Armenia belonged to the Georgian kingdoms, ruled by a branch of the Bagratid family, the same family that had once elevated medieval Armenia to greatness. In the west, the Seljuks still maintained their grasp on the kingdom. And in a handful of small provinces in the south, ethnic Armenians had managed to claw back some semblance of independence for their little group of people. But all that would change between around 1220 and 1240 when the Mongols decided that Armenia would be theirs.

The Mongol conquest of Armenia, however, did not take place with the steamroller efficiency that many other hapless countries had experienced when they fell to the wrath of the Mongols. It took twenty years and almost as much diplomatic negotiating as warfare; each move on the part of the Mongols was a carefully calculated strategic maneuver, brilliantly executed. The invasion of Armenia, which finally fell around 1240, was more proof than ever that Genghis Khan—for all his brutality—was more than just a terrorizing force of evil. He was a military genius, lauded in the East as much as he was feared and hated in the West.

* * * *

As Armenia was held in the icy grip of the Mongol hordes, the Kingdom of Armenian Cilicia continued to thrive on the Crusade-rich environment of the 13$^{th}$ century, so much so that it was soon no longer known as Cilicia. Instead, it was so densely populated by Armenians that it was given a new name: Lesser Armenia.

The Rubenid dynasty had intermarried with and been absorbed into the Hethumid dynasty in Lesser Armenia, and when the Mongols swept across Greater Armenia and captured much of Asia Minor, the king of Lesser Armenia, Hethum I, knew that his country would suffer the same fate if it dared to defy the Mongols. Instead, he formed an alliance with them, an act that may feel treacherous in retrospect but one that saved his country from being overrun the way Greater Armenia was. Hethum and his men fought in the Mongolian campaigns that continued across the Middle East.

But the Mongols were not as invincible as they appeared. Their campaigns would grind to a halt in the face of a class of warrior slaves whose loyalties lay with no one: the Mamluks.

An important part of Muslim armies, the Mamluks were property, but they were extremely valuable. Taken from their families as young boys, they were raised in the barracks, giving them no one to be loyal to except their owners and one another. Raised and trained for war and nothing else, the Mamluks fought with a professional kind of dedication, as their whole lives were devoted to battle. The Egyptian Mamluks were among the only soldiers who ever successfully stood against the Mongols, and they did so in the mid-13$^{th}$ century, drawing a firm eastern border of the Mongolian conquest. Even Genghis Khan did not get past them.

This had devastating consequences for Lesser Armenia, which was a powerful rival to the Muslim world, thanks to its control of the spice trade and also its support of the Crusades. The Mamluk leader demanded that Hethum switch his alliance from Mongolia to Egypt. Knowing that he was facing a tremendous foe, Hethum fled to the

Mongol court to beg for help. In his absence, the Mamluks invaded Lesser Armenia and conquered it, all but destroying the country in 1266.

An earthquake shattered whatever the Mamluks had left standing just two years later. And while it would cling to its status as a kingdom for a little over another century, albeit a shadow of its former self and constantly harried by the Muslim forces, Lesser Armenia's days were numbered. The Turkic and Mamluk armies eventually tore it up into pieces, and by the Mamluk invasion of 1375, Lesser Armenia was a kingdom no more. Its Armenian inhabitants fled to Cyprus, France, and other countries. The home that had sheltered them for hundreds of years was gone.

* * * *

In its long history, Armenia had faced many devastating conquerors. It had been trampled and torn down by ancient Rome, by Alexander the Great, and even by Genghis Khan. But one of the most dreaded—and the most legendary—men ever to claim Armenia's highlands as his own was Timur the Lame, better known in the West as Tamerlane.

During the 14th century, the spectacular power of the Mongols began to fade in the wake of Genghis Khan's death. Armenia might have been free, but the Mongols were briskly supplanted by a Turkic nation, the Chupanids, also spelled as the Chobanids.

Armenia had not been an independent kingdom since the time of the Bagratuni family. Even Lesser Armenia was gone now; the heart of the Armenian people was as oppressed as their physical bodies. Generations of Armenians did not know what it meant to be free, and they would not be free again for another five hundred years. The next conqueror who rose up against them was Tamerlane, and he devastated Armenia in a way that even this much-defeated people had never experienced before. For it was by the hand of Tamerlane that the first Turkish massacre of the Armenians was performed.

By the time he invaded Armenia and Georgia, Tamerlane had become a legend, a bogeyman that was all too real. Born in modern Uzbekistan, Tamerlane was a nobody, and a disabled one at that, as a childhood injury left his right side crippled. He grew up as a kind of amateur highwayman, mugging innocent travelers with his friends, despite the fact that his father was a wealthy minor noble, and his desire to conquer did not end there. By the year 1400, Tamerlane had beaten the messy tribes of his area into an unstoppable army, unifying a scattered region in much the same way as Genghis Khan had done. He had defeated both Persia and India, and he had proven himself more powerful even than the Mamluks. So, Armenia was no match for him. Tamerlane did not just invade the country: he utterly destroyed it. Witnesses described how he would destroy a thousand-year-old city in a single day, his forces even going so far as to dig up ancient fortifications, and his scorched-earth policy left nothing untouched. Nothing left alive.

As for the people, they suffered under Tamerlane as they had never suffered before. Men, women, children, Christians, pagans—it didn't matter to him. He just wanted them dead, all of them. The accounts of Tamerlane's massacre are absolutely chilling, as they describe how he had Armenians thrown from the city walls to their deaths in such numbers that the piles of corpses grew and grew to the extent that their dead bodies cushioned some of the last victims. It is difficult to comprehend the terror that those last victims must have experienced; lying there, their limbs broken, their skin crushed, upon a great pile of their fellow citizens, as they died slowly and tangled amid the corpses of their own countrymen.

What Tamerlane did to the Armenians was brutal. But it was just a taste, a brief foreshadowing of what was coming.

# Chapter 11 – The First Deportation

One of the races that Tamerlane would face in his bid to defeat the whole of Asia and Europe was also Turkic like him: the Ottomans. And long after Tamerlane's Timurid Empire had melted away into history, the Ottoman Turks would continue to build an empire that would last for centuries.

The Timurid Empire, founded by Tamerlane, effectively ended Mongol power. It controlled a vast stretch of Europe and Asia, including modern-day Iran, Afghanistan, Turkmenistan, Uzbekistan, Tajikistan, Iraq, India, Pakistan, Syria, and Armenia. Tamerlane's capital, Samarkand, was known as the "Center of the World," and it was here that Tamerlane proved himself to be a dedicated patron of the arts and culture—which is ironic considering how badly he had devastated Armenian culture. His conquests killed almost twenty million people, but his empire would not last for long. Like Alexander's, it was divided up after his death. By the beginning of the 16th century, the Timurid Empire was no more, although one of its branches, the Mughal Empire, would last in India until the mid-19th century.

With the Mongols and the Timurids gone, and the Holy Roman Empire already starting to lose power and crumble under its own weight, there was a vacuum of power in the Middle East and Asia Minor. That vacuum would be filled by a Turkish superpower that had already started making its presence felt in the time of Tamerlane.

The Ottoman Turks were born on the very doorstep of Armenia. Originating in the mountains of Anatolia, the Ottomans were little more than just another Turkish tribe, much like the Chupanids, who had lost their grip on Armenia by now; Armenia had become a battleground once again between rivaling tribes until the time of Mehmed II. Known as Mehmed the Conqueror, he transformed the Ottomans into more than just some little tribe. They became a nation and, later, an empire. Like most Turks, Mehmed and his people were Muslims. It was a crushing blow for all of Christianity—and an enormous triumph for the Islamic world—when Mehmed defeated Byzantium, now Constantinople. The ancient Byzantine Empire had already been weakened, and Mehmed's attack in 1453 was the nail in the coffin. He made Constantinople his own capital, and so, the Ottoman Empire was born.

Of course, for the hapless Armenians, this was not good. Mehmed conquered Cilicia and imprisoned the Armenian population that still lived there, which mostly consisted of lower-class people who had not been able to flee when it was first invaded by the Mamluks in the late 14th century. Mehmed moved many of them to Constantinople, where conditions proved to be so unbearable that thousands of Armenians undertook a migration to Bruges, Belgium. A diaspora community 30,000 strong thrives there to this day.

The Ottoman Empire continued to grow, especially during the rule of Suleiman the Magnificent. It reached its height in the 16th century, absorbing Syria, Egypt, Palestine, Bulgaria, Romania, Jordan, Lebanon, parts of Arabia and Africa, Hungary, and Greece, among others.

Yet even with the Byzantine, Timurid, and Mongol Empires out of the way, the Ottomans did not find themselves wholly unopposed as they entered the 16th and 17th centuries. Persia, which was devastated by Arabia in the 7th century, was about to rise again one more time. And this time, it would be more glorious than ever.

Claiming to be descendants of Tamerlane, the Safavid dynasty of Persia rose to power in 1501. Their rule would continue until the 18th century, ushering in the Golden Age of Persia and bringing Persia onto a collision course with the Ottoman Empire.

The Sasanid Persians had been Zoroastrians, but centuries of Arabic rule had converted Persia to Islam. Even since the days just after Muhammad, however, Islam itself had been divided into two sects: the Sunni Muslims and the Shi'ite Muslims. The Ottomans were Sunnis, as most Muslims are today. But the Persians were Shi'ites, and that made them worse than infidels in the eyes of the Ottomans. To make matters worse, the Safavids wanted to expand Persia once again into the mighty empire that it once had been, and the Ottomans were in the way. And, once again, Armenia would find itself caught in the crossfire.

The Ottoman-Persian Wars would rage for more than three hundred years, and in that time, Armenia would be beaten back and forth like a ping-pong ball between two players who cared nothing for the ball; they only cared about winning the game. For everyday Armenians, this was everything but a game. Life was a battleground, and no city was safe from one horde or the other that came trampling across the mountainside without regard for the people whose lives were being constantly uprooted, changed, or, routinely, ended. Yerevan itself, now the capital of Armenia, was passed back and forth seventeen times over the course of the wars.

To make matters worse, the Jelālī Revolts, a series of clashes once again between Sunni and Shi'ite Muslims, took place in Armenia and Anatolia around this time. Yet even with warring soldiers of all kinds of other faiths around them, the Armenians managed to cling to one aspect of their national identity: their faith. They remained staunchly Christian, even though this made both the Ottomans and the Persians treat them as somehow inferior. One example of how poorly the Ottomans treated Armenians was with something called the devshirme system, aptly nicknamed "blood tax." In this tax, boys from Christian villages in Armenia and its surroundings were kidnapped by the state, forcibly converted to Islam, and then made to serve the government for the rest of their lives.

Yet it was not the Ottomans who would subject Armenians to the greatest cruelty they suffered in the 16th century. It was the Persians.

* * * *

The Araxes River was swollen and hot and angry, water plunging between its banks like a wild animal bent on breaking its bonds. Its foaming waters roared even louder than the thunder of thousands of hooves and hundreds of thousands of feet, louder even than the crack of the cannons in the distance as 300,000 Armenian villagers tramped warily up to the bursting banks. The same river that had given the ancient Kura-Araxes people their name was now earning its own name of "fast-flowing." The waters were swift and deadly, and even knowing that there was an Ottoman horde on their heels, the villagers ground to a halt. They looked up at the soldiers accompanying them, unbelieving. On either side of the river, the wreckage of what had once been a bridge was barely visible. How were they supposed to get across the river?

Shah Abbās I the Great, the king of Safavid Persia, had not counted on having to flee back this way when he had ordered his armies to destroy the bridge behind them. He was a gifted military leader, a commander who had led his army to victory after victory against the Ottomans. He had believed that laying siege to Kars, an Armenian city, in 1604 would be just another victory. Only it wasn't. Abbas had no choice but to retreat, and his hard struggle against the Ottomans had taught him an even harder lesson: the only way to beat them was to leave them with nothing. He had to destroy every village that he left behind in order to avoid allowing the Ottomans to find resources in the rich highlands of Armenia.

Abbās' men had butchered the Armenians' animals. They had burned their homes and razed their villages and towns to the very ground, then burned the grass so that there was nothing left. They had told the Armenians that it was for their own good. They had told the Armenians to come with them for their own safety, to avoid being murdered by the Ottomans, and for a time, the Armenians had trusted them. The Persians were Muslims, but on the whole, Abbās had been tolerant of his Christian subjects so far.

But now, the king was desperate. He knew the Ottomans were in hot pursuit, and 300,000 milling villagers had slowed him down. Knowing that his fit soldiers on their strong horses would ford the river easily, Abbās ordered them to cross.

The Armenians knew they could not make it. Clutching their children close, they watched him with wide eyes. One of them—brave or foolish or perhaps just fed up and exhausted after what had already been a long march—tried to break ranks and flee back to what was left of his home. A gunshot rang out, and the man dropped dead in a pool of blood.

Trapped between the murderous Persians and the deadly river, the Armenians had no choice. They had to take their chances with the water—and those chances were slim. Old people and young children and the sick and simply those caught off guard by the icy, rushing waters found themselves overwhelmed in seconds. Soon, corpses were flowing through the river like flood debris, bumping against the living as they attempted to cross the raging water. Thousands of them perished in the Araxes that day, and it was just the beginning of what was to come.

During the long march through the middle of winter to the safety of Isfahan, a city in Persia, the Armenian villagers perished in the hundreds of thousands. Those who resisted the march were swiftly and brutally dispatched by the soldiers; those who did not die realized that no provisions had been made to feed them. The sound of thousands of crying children filled the air, following the marchers wherever they went like a clinging cloud of black mist. They died like flies, leaving behind a trail of withered, skeletal corpses. Those most desperate picked at those corpses, feeding on the human flesh in a bid to simply survive.

By the time the march was over, less than 150,000 of those villagers remained alive. Even though Abbās had not directly attacked the Armenians as a people, he had wrought the same atrocities on them as Tamerlane and Genghis Khan.

The Safavids had not treated the Armenians well, but like many empires that had come and gone before them, they would not last forever. Albeit clinging on to Eastern Armenia for another two hundred years, the Safavid Empire began to decline in the 18th century as both the Ottomans and Russia fought against it. By 1828, Armenia was once again divided among two conquering kingdoms: Western Armenia belonging to the Muslim Ottomans and Eastern Armenia to the Christian Russians. The Safavid Empire was no more, having collapsed in 1736.

The majority of ethnic Armenians were now living in the vast and bloated Ottoman Empire as the 19$^{th}$ century wore on. Suffice it to say that the Ottomans did not treat them well. As religious freedom became more of a theme across the globe, the Ottomans continued to use the millet system—a way of dividing people along racial and religious lines and taxing them accordingly. Armenians, who still clung constantly to Christianity, were considered to be some of the most inferior people in the empire. They were taxed far more heavily than their Muslim counterparts. Somehow, though, the Armenians managed to thrive within the empire, their numbers reaching an all-time high. They were used to oppression; they had endured it for generations, and they knew how to survive—and even how to succeed—without the freedoms that so much of the world took for granted.

The Ottomans had taken their children. The Persians had taken their lives. But what Armenia had suffered was nothing in comparison to what was coming next. They would be the first nation to endure the greatest crime of all: genocide.

# Chapter 12 – Genocide

Hapless Armenians undertake a forced march

*https://commons.wikimedia.org/wiki/File:Column_of_deportees_walking_through_Harput_vilay
et_during_the_Armenian_genocide.jpg*

---

The screams of the young woman in labor echoed across the desert. They were ripping sounds, holding so much more than the primal agony of childbirth. They shredded the air with a razor-sharp terror, bursting with loneliness, with desperation. The young girl walking beside the horse had heard women in labor before in the rural village that had once been her world, a village that felt like it was a thousand years away now. It sounded painful, but it also sounded like something of hope, as if even in that agony, an expectant mother knew that a new life was being brought forth. But the girl's sister screamed in simple pain. There was no hope in her voice. There was no hope in the barren landscape through which the long ribbon of desolate marchers moved. There was no hope in their empty eyes as they gazed down at the ground at their feet, avoiding the bloodstains and the corpses and the places where others had squatted down to relieve themselves, having nowhere else to go. There was no hope in the way they walked with their slumped shoulders, not even looking up as the woman's shrieks continued to reverberate from dune to dune across the Syrian Desert. There was not even interest because her screams were not the only ones to resound through this hopeless wilderness. Here, a child was crying, begging for food; there, a baby moaning in one steady monotone, as it had been doing for days, as it would not do for much longer; and not far away, a girl was being raped, a man butchered with a blade, a mother crumbling down in grief by the side of her child.

There were worse reasons to scream than childbirth. But could there be a worse childbirth than this young mother was enduring? The soldiers had refused to let her stop. One, kinder than the others (the others might simply have butchered her), had lifted her onto his horse. And now, on that moving animal, she was bringing a baby girl out into the world.

A world that hated them. A world that had rejected them.

This eyewitness account was told in abrupt and simple terms by a young girl who was only twelve years old when she was ripped from her home. She was lucky enough to survive the genocide, but around one million Armenians were not so lucky.

By the late 19$^{th}$ century, Armenia had endured more than can really be believed. The fact that the Armenians still had a national and cultural identity—one that was stronger than ever as the Christian Armenian communities lived a life so separate from their Turkish neighbors—is almost surprising, considering what they had been through so far. Yet the darkest period in Armenian history was yet to come. The genocide would soon begin.

The first taste of this level of destruction occurred in 1894. The Ottoman Empire was in decline, and its sultan, Abdul Hamid II, was well aware of this fact. An exceptionally paranoid and corrupt ruler, Abdul Hamid feared nothing more than losing parts of the empire, and the fact that it was crumbling at the edges terrified him. Instead of working to unite the empire, however, he struck out at an ethnic minority that posed little threat to him: the Armenians. Although the Armenian Revolutionary Federation (ARF) had caused some rebellions in parts of the country, most of the Armenian people were fairly peace-loving, as no doubt were many of the Muslim Turks. But Abdul Hamid continued to tell all who would listen that the Armenians were dangerous, that they were going to be the downfall of the empire. His brainwashing inevitably began to take effect, and the Turks began to regard their Armenian neighbors with growing suspicion.

Things came to a head in the Susan region when taxes were raised and a small group of Armenians refused to pay up. There is no record that these people were at all violent, but Abdul Hamid's men did not need to see any violence to strike first. Tensions erupted, and soldiers opened fire on the civilian Armenians. It was only the first of several waves of killings between 1894 and 1896, with Turkish soldiers and even some civilians turning against the Armenians. Carrying weapons was illegal if you were Armenian; these people were defenseless, and they were slaughtered like cattle. Around 300,000 Armenians died during this time, in what is called the Hamidian massacres.

With eerie and appalling familiarity, another spate of killings erupted in 1909. By then, the Young Turks—a progressive group of revolutionaries with visions for a more modern and diplomatic Ottoman Empire—had risen up to overthrow Abdul Hamid and take hold of the government in 1908. The Young Turk Revolution was a day so joyous that Muslims and Christians had embraced each other on the streets, a day where Armenians and Turks stood side by side with the hope of equality at last. That hope was dimmed in April 1909. Supporters of Abdul Hamid staged a revolt, and instead of fighting the Turks, they fought the Armenians, who could not fight back. In the city of Adana, part of what had once been the Armenian Kingdom of Cilicia, 30,000 Armenians were ruthlessly murdered. American missionaries, for their part, suffered alongside them.

But the Adana and Hamidian massacres, devastating though they were, were nothing compared to the genocide proper.

When the Young Turks regained control over the empire after the Adana massacre, there was a vague hope that perhaps things would be better with them in charge. It was a useless, misplaced hope. Instead of working toward the unity of a diverse empire, the Young Turks—now the leaders of the Committee of Union and Progress, or CUP, the leading political party of the Ottomans—decided that there was only one way to present a united front to a world on the brink of World War I. This was "Turkification": the presentation of Turkish identity that was seen as being utterly vital to the survival of the empire. Accordingly, anyone who was not Turkish—anyone who was, for example, Armenian—was nothing short of a direct threat to the Ottoman Empire's survival.

While the Turkification campaign proved disastrous for religious and ethnic minorities, the Young Turks' fear, albeit misplaced, was understandable. Tensions across the globe had never been higher, and for a failing empire, a world war could spell disaster. But a world war was coming. In desperate need of a strong ally, when the First World War erupted in 1914, the Ottomans entered in it on the side of their allies, Germany and the Austro-Hungarian Empire. Less understandable was the Ottomans' next decision: to declare war not only on Germany's enemies but also on all Christians excepting the Germans. For the Ottomans, the "Great War" was even more than a world war. It was a holy one.

Considering there had been practically no repercussions for the perpetrators of the Adana and Hamidian massacres, it is unsurprising that the Armenians quickly became the perceived public enemy of the Ottoman Empire. Having weathered rebellions in the Balkans, and having lost the Balkan Wars with devastating consequences for the empire, the Ottoman soldiers viewed the Armenians as being potentially dangerous. But their government blew this suspicion way out of proportion. With the Ottoman borders under attack, the Turks turned their attention instead to their own population, electing to eradicate an entire race.

The Armenian Genocide began on April 24th, 1915, when hundreds of Armenian intellectuals were arrested, imprisoned, and, later, deported. These were middle- to upper-class people who contributed to Ottoman society as scientists, artists, writers, and thinkers; it is probable that all of them were innocent of any kind of rebellion. Yet they soon found themselves on a forced march across the Syrian Desert, to be expelled from the bowels of the empire and vomited up like something poisonous even though they posed no threat.

Over the next seven years, hundreds of thousands of Armenians would be expelled from their homes, and the cruelty did not end with deportation. These people were butchered. Even helpless orphans were ordered to be killed as the Ottoman treatment of the Armenians quickly blossomed into a full-blown attempt to exterminate the entire race once and for all. As persecuted as the Armenians had been for centuries, they had never suffered like this.

They were killed by the thousands in almost every way imaginable. Shot on the death marches across the desert. Gutted with swords in gruesome ways in order to frighten those who yet survived. Starved. Beaten. Raped. In one awful instance, five thousand were gathered together, tied to a pile of dry grass, and burned to death, their shrieks echoing across the homeland where their people had lived for untold thousands of years. The children were inoculated with blood that was infected with typhus; the people were overdosed on morphine, gassed, or herded onto ships and then thrown overboard within sight of the city of Trebizond. Thousands of children were sold off as slaves—sometimes sex slaves—to Muslim households. And while many Muslim civilians did their part in a bid to save the Armenians (with some accounts telling of Muslim men marrying whole groups of Armenian women to save them from certain death), some turned on their own neighbors as they had done in the Hamidian and Adana massacres and butchered them in the streets.

By 1922, the Armenian population had been utterly decimated. There had been around 1.5 million Armenians in the empire prior to 1915. When the genocide finally ended as World War I came to a close and the world woke up to the reality of what had taken place, there were only 388,000 left. About three-quarters of the Armenian population was dead. For every person left alive, three were gone. For every family of four, only one was left. Those who had lived were all grieving the loss of three-quarters of the people they knew, and a terrible, gaping wound was left where those people once had been, as Muslim families moved into the homes from which the Armenians had been so forcefully wrested.

The Armenian Genocide was a chapter of history that cannot, and will not, be forgotten —despite the best efforts of even the modern Turkish government. Even to this very day, Turkey refuses to admit that what occurred was truly genocide, even though experts in this grave field widely accept that the events of 1915 to 1922 were genocide. In fact, it is illegal in Turkey to even mention what was done to the Armenians, and to this day, many countries—including the US—do not officially recognize the genocide. The Holocaust is common knowledge; the Armenian Genocide is obscure history, in part thanks to Turkey's denial of its historical sins.

# Chapter 13 – Freedom at Last

General Drastamat Kanayan, "Dro" to friends and to history, had wanted to be a soldier ever since he was a little boy. As a kid, he would play hooky to watch the Russian soldiers at the barracks near his home. Their drills and exercises fascinated him, and as yet another Armenian child living under the control of a foreign empire, perhaps something about their force and control appealed to his young heart. At least Russian Armenians were not persecuted for their religion as they were in the Ottoman Empire, but they were still a long way from being free.

Yet fighting alongside them still seemed better than living the ordinary life that Dro's time at school was leading him toward. Noticing that his son was hopeless in school, Dro's father sent him to the military school in Yerevan. The boy's grades barely improved, but his love for all things military grew nothing short of insatiable. It was a logical next step to become a soldier after graduation. It was all he had ever wanted to do.

And he had never truly desired to be a Russian soldier. He wanted to be an Armenian one, so much so that he secretly joined an underground youth movement opposing Russian rule. Nothing ever came of the movement, but it inspired Dro's heart, and in all the years since—years spent fighting the First World War on the Russian side—he had not let go of that inspiration.

Yet today, now, as he looked out over the battlefield thrown wide before him, Dro was not so sure that he really was cut out for the role in which history had cast him. He had wanted to fight for his people ever since he was a kid, but perhaps he had not realized how high the stakes could become. On the outskirts of Sardarapat, less than twenty miles from his home in Yerevan, Dro was watching the advance of an army that he knew his forces could not hope to beat. Ten thousand Ottomans. Three thousand Kurdish cavalry, legendary for their outrageous bloodthirst. Forty great cannons, and at any moment, their devastating crack would ring out across the mountains and rain death upon the group of Armenians at Dro's side. There were 9,000 of them; they were not as badly outnumbered as they could have been, but the Ottomans were trained soldiers, veterans of four years of the world war. And the Armenians...Dro scanned his ranks, letting out a little sigh. There were a handful of real soldiers, of course, but most of the people standing by his side were nobodies. Blacksmiths and butchers. Farmers and grocers. They were armed with whatever he and his men were able to rustle up on such short notice. How could they hope to stand against the Ottomans?

He looked further back, beyond the ranks of his men, toward the roads leading to Yerevan, and they were black with carts and people. Water buffalo and donkeys and even the sagging old shapes of skinny dairy cows were harnessed to those carts, women and little children driving the beasts up to the army, and the carts were piled high with everything that they could get their hands on: food, water, medical supplies, crude weaponry. Dro's heart flipped over in his chest. This was the Armenian people. They were all standing with him, behind him, watching a purely Armenian army go out to battle for its own people for the first time in centuries. The people were looking up at him like he was Tigranes the Great, or Hayk, or some hero. Some hero who could rebuild the glory days of Urartu and the Armenian Empire.

Dro raised his chin and watched the Ottomans coming, and he knew that the odds were slim. But he also knew that he had to try. No one was coming to rescue Armenia.

It was time for them to rescue themselves.

* * * *

As the genocide raged in the Ottoman Empire, there was only one region of historic Armenia that could still be considered safe: the tiny slice of Eastern Armenia that had remained under the control of the Russian Empire. Albeit a small portion of the once-mighty country, Eastern Armenia was the very heart of the ancient land, containing Mount Ararat and the once-capital, Yerevan. It was still considered a Russian protectorate, and with the tremendous power of the Russian army defending it, it was the one place where the Armenians could go and the Ottomans could not follow.

Refugees streamed into Eastern Armenia as the genocide continued unabated. The Russians had seized Armenian Church property and made lives difficult for their Armenian subjects, but at least they had not murdered a million of them. Anything would be better than the Ottomans.

But at the eleventh hour, shortly after the Bolsheviks seized power in Moscow, Russia pulled out. The Russian troops that had been guarding hundreds of thousands of refugees in Eastern Armenia simply packed up and headed back home upon Bolshevik orders, leaving the Armenians utterly defenseless against the invading masses of the Ottoman army. It was May 1918; World War I had all but destroyed

Europe, and each country was scrambling wildly to hold on to its own freedom. No one was coming to save the Armenians. What was left of them, at least.

If the Battle of Sardarapat, which took place in late May 1918, had turned out differently, there would be no Armenia on the map today. In fact, the very Armenian race may have been as wholly exterminated as the Ottomans had hoped. The vast majority of the surviving Armenian population was living in Eastern Armenia, and if the Ottomans overran it, they would no doubt subject them to the same treatment as their Western cousin. Dro and his men were not just fighting for independence—they were fighting for the very survival of their own race. The stakes had never been higher.

But May 28th, 1918, would go down in history as the day that Armenia was set free once again. Because that was the day that the ragged Armenian army, composed mostly of volunteers, drew a line in the sand and said, "This far and no farther." That was the day that the borders of modern Armenia were drawn, the day that the Armenian people were saved not by the Romans or the Byzantine Empire or the Mongols but by themselves, their own people, depleted of their resources, stripped of their pride, their identity trampled, their race decimated, their allies vanished. They had nothing except the burning courage that had kept them clinging on to their faith, to their culture, to who they were. They had nothing but their identity, and on that day, their identity was enough. Armenia was forced to stand for itself. And stand it did.

The Battle of Sardarapat was Armenia's rebirth, a baptism in blood, as Dro and the rest of the generals and barefoot volunteers that surrounded him held back the Ottomans on the banks of the Araxes, the selfsame river where the Persians had drowned thousands of Armenians on the eve of the very first mass killing in the 17th century. But not today. Today the Ottomans fell in untold numbers, and the

Armenians fought back, and they won.

The Ottoman Empire was forced into a disorganized retreat, their armies fleeing back into their own lands. Eastern Armenia would never see Turkish rule again. And while the genocide would continue in Western Armenia for another four years, those who managed to flee to the mountains around Yerevan were saved. The Armenian race would live on, not so much surviving as being resurrected in the blazing light of Sardarapat.

* * * *

May 28th, 1918, became the date commemorated for the founding of the First Republic of Armenia. Dro was its defense minister; his fellow general, Tovmas Nazarbekian, became the commander-in-chief. It was the first time in centuries that Armenia would be independent, even if it was just a tiny slice of Armenia for now.

This independence would be short-lived, but it was incredible while it lasted. The Ottoman Empire and its allies ended World War I in defeat, and it was the nail in the coffin for the declining empire. Its territories were granted independence or divided among the conquering nations; the Republic of Armenia was one of those who became independent, and on October 30th, 1918, it was able to annex Western Armenia as well. The ancient nation was whole once more. And in 1922, the Ottoman Empire finally breathed its last, reemerging as the Republic of Turkey in 1923. It was only when the Ottoman Empire ended that the genocide stopped, too.

For two years, the Republic of Armenia started to try and piece together a decimated country. How do you rebuild a nation with three-quarters of its population dead? Courageous volunteers, some from across the globe, began to work to rescue the women and children that had been kidnapped and enslaved during the genocide, and slowly, the Republic of Armenia began to take form. Sadly, it would not last for long.

The Bolsheviks that had so easily abandoned Armenia to its fate were suddenly becoming interested in the nation once more, now that it was so much larger and proving that it was still worth something, despite the devastation that it had suffered. The Armenian Soviet Socialist Republic was established as a political organization in December 1920, and it opposed the Republic of Armenia, alongside the Russians and Turkey. With grisly déjà vu, Armenia was caught in the crossfire of Turkey and the Soviet Union, just like it had been so many times during its history. The First Republic of Armenia couldn't hope to stand against the USSR-backed Armenian Soviet Socialist Republic. The Russians took the east, the Turks took the west, and Eastern Armenia became a part of the Soviet Union in 1923. As for Western Armenia, it remains a part of Turkey to this day, and barely a handful of ethnic Armenians still live there. The genocide was successful in removing the Armenian question from Western Armenia entirely.

Life in Armenia under the Soviet Union became rapidly unbearable. The Turks had belittled and looked down on Armenians for their faith, and the Russians arrested them for it. Joseph Stalin's bid to eradicate religion entirely within the Soviet Union was an unspeakable cruelty to many Armenians, for whom their beloved faith was the only thing they had left after surviving the genocide. To some among them, taking away Christianity may have felt like an even worse crime than genocide itself. The faith still survived, however, as Christians met in secret to hide the fact that they still worshiped in defiance of Stalin.

Muslim Armenians, of whom there were by this time a significant number, were not exempt from this cruelty, either. They suffered right alongside their Christian counterparts; thousands of them were deported from Georgia to Uzbekistan in 1944.

But like all of the empires that had controlled Armenia, the Soviet Union would not last forever. Despite emerging from World War II more powerful than ever before, and becoming a looming threat to the capitalist world during the long era of tensions known as the Cold War, the Soviet Union began to decline in the late 20$^{th}$ century. By 1991, the Berlin Wall came crashing down, and the Soviet Union died just like all of those old empires that had tried to make Armenia theirs.

The Romans, the Byzantines, the Mongols, the Arabs, the Parthians, the Persians, the Timurids, the Ottomans, the Soviets—they had all been powerful once, and they had all faded out of Armenia's history. But this tiny country, having suffered so much, having endured more than can be imagined, was still holding on. And for the first time in many, many years, it was free.

# Chapter 14 – A Study in Velvet

A snow-capped Mount Ararat in the distance

Serzh Sargsyan was nervous, a strange fact considering that he had been involved in politics since he was just a twenty-something in the 70s. Now a hawk-eyed man with an imposing presence and a crop of snow-white hair, Sargsyan walked into the meeting room on April 22$^{nd}$, 2018, with an attempt at haughtiness. He had been the prime minister of Armenia, had been the president for ten years, and had just been elected as prime minister once again. Surely, of all the people of Armenia, Sargsyan had nothing to fear. Yet there was something in his darting dark eyes, in the way he smoothed down his shiny gray suit, that suggested that the pride in his bearing hid a note of fear.

It would have been deeply strange for Sargsyan to feel fear here and now. The room was large and empty except for a significant gaggle of camera-toting journalists, a cluster of microphones, and a slightly chubby middle-aged man in a camo T-shirt and an Adidas ball cap sitting on a chair by the microphones. This man, Nikol Pashinyan, a political nobody (except for the fact that he had been imprisoned for his rebellious writings) and the head of a minuscule political party named the Civil Contract, was himself looking a little wary. He fiddled with the straps of his rucksack as Sargsyan took his place across from him.

Sargsyan regarded Pashinyan for a moment, then spoke in a falsely jovial tone. He thanked Pashinyan for finally agreeing to meet with him after several days of attempting to make contact. Pashinyan's eyes were everywhere except on Sargsyan, perhaps a little overwhelmed. He had started his quiet walk from his home in Gyumri a little over three weeks earlier. Since then, pacing through the streets of Armenia, he had made his way to Yerevan. He was worn and travel-stained and tired, but he had succeeded in his objective: an audience with the prime minister, whose election had sparked Pashinyan's peaceful march. He had only agreed to speak to Sargsyan regarding his resignation as prime minister, but it would soon be clear that Sargsyan had no intentions to do so.

Having thanked Pashinyan for his presence, Sargsyan turned to the journalists and gave them a wide, white smile. He told Pashinyan cheerfully that he was not sure how to negotiate in front of so many people—a move that hinted at the ten years of corruption that had characterized his time as commander-in-chief of Armenia.

Pashinyan's face was still nervous, but his voice was calm and steady when he spoke up. "I came here to discuss the conditions of your resignation."

Sargsyan scoffed. He told Pashinyan that made their conversation something different from a resignation—it made it blackmail. "You did not learn the lesson of March 1$^{st}$," he stated furiously.

Pashinyan looked up then, and his eyes flashed. March 1$^{st}$, 2008. The day of Sargsyan's election as president, and the day that protests erupted all across Yerevan as the public made it clear that they knew the election had been rigged. Ten people had died when the police had opened fire on the protesters. Pashinyan had been there; he had been arrested for being there and had become a political prisoner for years. He knew that Sargsyan's words were a thinly veiled threat to the hundreds of peaceful protesters across Yerevan now, all on strike in a bid to support Pashinyan.

"The whole responsibility is on you," Sargsyan told the younger man, a bid to make him a scapegoat for the bloodbath that he was determined to make this protest into. "Choose."

Pashinyan's voice did not rise. "Nobody can talk with us in the language of threats," he said calmly. "The power in the Republic of Armenia transferred to the people."

At that, Sargsyan laughed out loud. "The group which got seven or eight percent in the election has not the right to talk in the name of a nation," he said sharply.

It was true that Pashinyan's party had been barely a blip on the radar in the recent elections, but Pashinyan knew that the world was changing. As Sargsyan ranted about how he did not want to continue the conversation, Pashinyan cast his eyes to the floor. "Goodbye," he said. Then, sharper, "Goodbye!"

Sargsyan gave him a last angry glare. He launched to his feet and strode from the room, leaving Pashinyan to address the journalists with a quiet confidence. A confidence that was not misplaced. In just a few weeks, Pashinyan's words would be proven true. And not a single shot would be fired.

The truth was that Pashinyan was right. March 1ˢᵗ, 2008, had seen an Armenia still wet behind the ears from the birth of its independence. Its military and police force had fired on the protesting crowds on Sargsyan's order, not questioning his authority. But the ten years that passed had begun to remind the Armenians that they could be more than this. They *would* be more than this. As the protest—always utterly peaceful—gathered strength, Sargsyan became more and more nervous. But the protesters never turned violent. There was no looting; Pashinyan had commanded as much. There was no chaos. And at ten every evening, the protesters all went home, only to return fresh-faced the next morning and peacefully voice the fact that they were done with corruption.

When Sargsyan demanded that the police should stop them, he realized the extent of Pashinyan's revolution because none of the officers would listen to him anymore. The corrupt leader had no one left to follow him, and he knew he was beaten. By May 8ᵗʰ, Nikol Pashinyan, the nobody, had become the president of Armenia. His protests became known as the Velvet Revolution for their gentleness.

* * * *

The Republic of Armenia had been plagued by corruption ever since its first election on October 17ᵗʰ, 1991. But in the early days of the republic, there were much bigger issues to deal with, and the Nagorno-Karabakh War was chief among them.

The Nagorno-Karabakh War started back in the time of Stalin when swathes of ancient Armenia were given to modern-day Azerbaijan instead of to the ethnic Armenians living in Eastern Armenia. This immediately sparked discontent in Armenia, especially considering that tempers were still simmering about the genocide, as the Azerbaijani populating the region were a Turkic people that bore many similarities to the Ottoman Turks who had brought so much grief to the Armenians. At first, the powerful Soviet Union was able to keep Azerbaijan and Armenia from actually coming to blows over the issue—neither of the smaller countries was willing to get on the USSR's nerves too much. But as the Soviet Union's power began to decline in the 1980s, the enclave of Nagorno-Karabakh became the topic of heated arguments between Armenia and Azerbaijan. The problem was not diplomatically resolved, and so, resentment spilled over, and when the people of Nagorno-Karabakh itself voted to join Armenia in 1988, conflict broke out in the region.

For the next six years, fierce fighting continued between the two regions. The collapse of the Soviet Union in 1991, which allowed Armenia and Azerbaijan to gain independence, only briefly slowed down the war. It continued unabated until 1994 when both countries found themselves struggling internally and depleted of resources. Russia stepped in one last time to negotiate a ceasefire that was agreed on May 12th, 1994. At the time, although the war could have gone either way, Armenia undeniably had the upper hand. For the first time in centuries, the little nation was proving itself in warfare.

It was not with violence, however, that Armenia would ultimately solve its problems. As discontent broke out over the series of corrupt presidents and prime ministers that plagued the republic's early years, there were still several instances of violence. The first was on October 27th, 1999, when a group of gunmen entered Parliament and shot the very popular prime minister, who was looking like he was about to turn the country around, dead. The corrupt president, Robert Kocharyan, was conveniently left unhurt. The widespread protests of 2008 that Sargsyan mentioned in his not-so-subtle threat to Pashinyan were another example of Armenia's struggle to find its way out of a history of violence.

Another tragic incident of violence took place in 2015 in what has become known as the Gyumri massacre. It might not have taken hundreds of thousands of lives like the killings that happened a century earlier, but the grisly killing of the entire Avetisyan family—including a toddler and an infant boy—shocked the entire nation. This murder, however, was unlikely to be politically motivated, as the family was just an ordinary, relatively harmless family. The suspect, a teenage Russian soldier with a learning disability, was returned to Russia to stand trial. His motives remain unclear, although conspiracy theories abound.

Three years later, while the latest and most power-hungry in a string of corrupt leaders—Serzh Sargsyan—was in charge of Armenia, Gyumri would once again see history change. But this time, there would be no blood, bullets, or broken glass. There would be no brutal murders. There would be no rapes or gassings or drownings or starving. There would be walking, but this time, it would be done in hope. This time, there would be no Turkish soldiers prodding the weak onward to their deaths. This time, an Armenian man would toss a rucksack on his shoulders and start pacing along the streets, a growing crowd of people following him of their own volition. This time, they would laugh and talk. There would be no screams. There would be no silence. There would be not so much as a thrown stone.

In the Velvet Revolution, the Armenians would take control of their own lives, their own destinies. And they would show the whole of history the power of the Armenian spirit.

# Conclusion

In hearing the stories of modern-day Armenians—those who only know the genocide second- or third-hand from the voices of their great-grandparents—a common thread of wariness rings through each tale. This is a people that has suffered enormously, and not just this single generation. Armenians have been suffering ever since the Medes overthrew Urartu nearly three thousand years ago. They have suffered in almost every way conceivable, at the hands of almost any empire you care to name.

Yet, at the same time, there is something robust in their eyes and words. Something fearless, a glimmer of that tenacity that had Hayk draw back his bow on the shores of Lake Van, a spark of the vision that drove Tigranes the Great to build the Armenian Empire. There is a willingness there to buckle down and work hard. This is a people that are afraid to trust, a people that have seen too much and suffered far too many evils. But this is also a people ready for a new beginning. A people who feel responsible for their own fate.

What has changed since the days that a disheartened Armenia allowed itself to be tossed back and forth between Rome and Parthia, the Byzantines and the Sasanids, Turkey and Russia? The change was forged on the flanks of the mountains surrounding Sardarapat, where a group of Armenian volunteers grabbed whatever weapons they could find and made a final stand against the oncoming Ottomans. In the face of genocide, the very destruction of their people, Armenians stood together to cry no more. They put the Ottomans to flight, and they realized that they alone were responsible for their own people.

So, when Serzh Sargsyan told Nikol Pashinyan that the responsibility was his own, Pashinyan was as ready for it as Drastamat Kanayan had been at Sardarapat. At Sardarapat, the Armenians underwent a messy rebirth in blood and agony. But starting in Gyumri and undertaking the long walk to Yerevan, this people have proven something even more powerful. They have proven that a nation can heal from even the most devastating crime of all, genocide.

It remains to be seen whether Pashinyan's government really will bring about the hope that Armenians have for the future. Yet even if it does not, one gets the feeling looking into the eyes of the Armenians that this people will survive. In fact, they will do more than survive. Surviving was what they did during the genocide. Today, with a revolution of peace, with a spirit of hope and courage, they will do so much more than that. They will thrive.

And they might just show the rest of the world how to do that, against all the odds.

# Part 2: The Armenian Genocide

*A Captivating Guide to the Massacre of the Armenians by the Turks of the Ottoman Empire*

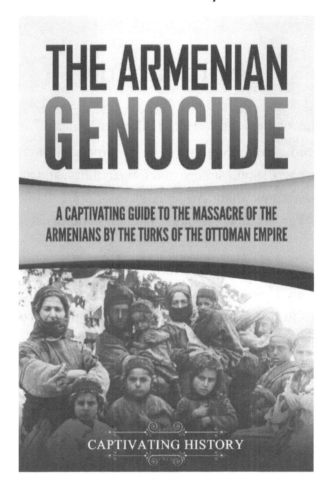

# Introduction

"Eat up! Think of the poor starving children in Armenia."

These words, commonly spoken in American households one hundred years ago, sound strange and foreign today. In fact, many of us might not even know where Armenia is. But during the horrors of the First World War, arguably no nation suffered as desperately as Armenia did.

The persecution of the Jewish during the Second World War, known worldwide as the Holocaust, is still very much present in global memory; a fact perhaps in part made possible by the widespread recognition that Germany recognizes its past mistakes. While politicians and civilians alike commemorate the deaths of roughly six million Jews from 1933 to 1945, the world has begun to forget a genocide that occurred twenty years before WWII started. And part of that may be because the nation that perpetrated it—modern-day Turkey—refuses to acknowledge that the genocide happened at all.

During 1915 to 1923, one and a half million Armenian people were deported and killed in the most appalling ways comprehensible. They were ripped from their homes (in a land where they had lived for longer than history can tell, a land so old that many speculate it was the site of the biblical Garden of Eden) and sent off on death marches across the blistering Syrian Desert. They were shot on the thresholds of the houses where they were raising their children. They were butchered with swords in gruesome ways in order to dishearten those left alive. They were starved in concentration camps, they were burned and drowned and beaten to death by the thousands, and then their corpses were stripped naked and left to rot in the open air. They were overdosed with morphine. They were injected with infected blood. They were cast overboard into the frigid Black Sea. They were gassed. They were raped. They were abducted and sold as slaves.

In short, the Ottoman Empire under the Three Pashas made every possible attempt to exterminate the Armenian race with such fervor that their actions would inspire the creation of the very word that now defines the greatest crime that can be perpetrated against a civilization: genocide. Yet today, the Armenian Genocide is an event that has melted out of the collective consciousness. It is an event that has repercussions extending to the modern day and is an event that should never be forgotten.

Do you know about the Armenians? Do you really know? Let this book show you, walking in the footsteps of the Armenian people starting in ancient times when they became the first officially Christian nation and started a precedent of having a strong national identity. Let it walk you through the oppressed lives of the Armenians during the Ottoman Empire. Let it stand you in their shoes as the first wave of genocide hits them. Let it make you a witness to their terrible suffering.

And let it give you hope. For the Armenians died, and they suffered, and they were mistreated in a way that can hardly be comprehended, but they did one thing more than anything else.

They survived.

# Chapter 1 – The Armenian Problem

The ancient scriptures tell the story of Noah, an old man who believed passionately in a god who'd been forgotten by the rest of the world. As the world was plunged into sin and darkness, Noah and his family alone listened for the light. When he was told that the world would be purged by means of a great and deadly flood, Noah knew that he alone would be spared but only if he built an ark: a gigantic wooden ship in which he and his family could shelter through the coming storm. And so, famously, Noah and his family boarded the ark alongside two of each kind of animal, and then it began to rain.

When the forty days and forty nights of rain had ceased, the earth was covered in water, the ark helplessly afloat on a flooded world. Noah and his family would drift for days until, at last, the ark ran aground. When the water finally cleared, they discovered that they had landed on the summit of a great mountain: Mount Ararat.

Today, Mount Ararat overlooks the sprawling city of Yerevan, the capital of Armenia—one of the oldest civilizations in the world. The genocide that would take place in the very shadow of the revered mountain is a terrible bloodstain on the face of a long and illustrious history that dates back many thousands of years.

* * * *

Modern-day Armenia is a small, landlocked country bordered by Turkey, Georgia, Azerbaijan, and Iran. Its towering mountains and deep valleys, cut from the landscape by swift-flowing rivers, have been the setting for millennia of human history.

People have been living in Armenia for so long that some traditions have identified it as the location of the biblical Garden of Eden, and science has discovered evidence of the most ancient human civilizations within its borders. Armenic Sumerian records dating back more than four thousand years suggests that Armenia may have been the first home of humanity.

The ancient land of Armenia was far larger than its modern-day equivalent. Encompassing much of its modern-day neighbors, ancient Armenia was a target for the Persians. Armenians are first mentioned by that name in Greek texts from around the 7$^{th}$ century BCE. Its scattered tribes were conquered under Alexander the Great in 331. It rose to prominence around the 1$^{st}$ century BCE when it was ruled by arguably its greatest king, Tigranes II. However, shortly after Tigranes' reign ended in 55 BCE, it was conquered again—this time by the greatest power of the ancient world: Rome.

Rome would continue to rule Armenia for centuries, although it had its own king and was relatively independent of the old, great empire, apart from it being used as a battlefield in Rome's continual struggles with the Parthians, who were from modern-day Iran. In fact, it was a Parthian king that would briefly overthrow the Romans in 53 CE, prompting a struggle over Armenian territory until a Roman emperor, Nero, made peace by crowning the Parthian leader—Tiridates I—king of Armenia, but he would also be a vassal to Rome.

It was Tiridates III, a descendant of Tiridates I, who would change the course of Armenian history. Its tribes would be united under one faith, a new and strange faith that was spreading like wildfire on the bare feet of its disciples throughout the ancient world. Little did he know what repercussions this simple act would have on the history of his people in a little less than two thousand years.

* * * *

For centuries, Armenian tribes had practiced polytheism, like many of the other ancient peoples surrounding them—including the Romans, who had been Armenia's ruler and strongest ally for hundreds of years by the end of the $3^{rd}$ century CE. Yet ever since the ancient apostle Paul had come to Antioch, rumors of a new faith had been spreading throughout the land. This faith was Christianity, and it was still in its very infancy, yet it captured the hearts of the Armenians.

By this point, Armenia was being ruled by Tiridates III but only with the help of Diocletian, the Roman emperor. The Persians had invaded and seized Armenia, assassinating Tiridates' father in the process, and only the imperial army had been able to drive them out and place Tiridates III on his rightful throne. He had formed a powerful alliance with Diocletian, and the two were on good terms.

He was not on good terms, however, with the noble families that had been involved in his father's assassination. These families faced punishment for the conspiracy, except for one young member: Grigor, known in English history as Gregory.

The story of St. Gregory the Illuminator is so old that it is part history and part tradition, but the version that follows is largely taken from a contemporary history by Agathangelos. The tale tells how his nurse, a

Christian lady, had carried him off to safety as a mere baby and raised him as her own. When Tiridates III retook the throne, Gregory was consumed with guilt for what his father had done. He was driven by a desire to atone for his father's sins, and he hoped to do so by bringing what he perceived to be the greatest gift of all to the country his father had betrayed: the Christian faith.

Joining Tiridates' court, Gregory quickly discovered that this would not be as easy as he'd hoped. Like the majority of the country, Tiridates was a pagan, and he expected his court to worship the same gods as he did. When Gregory refused to bow down to Tiridates' gods, the king was outraged that a mere palace functionary would dare to defy his king. He had Gregory tortured and then hurled into the deep, dark prison of Khor Virap, which means "pit of oblivion." Nobody ever came back from that dank pit, which stood in the very shadow of Mount Ararat.

Enraged, Tiridates—right alongside Diocletian—launched a series of persecutions against the Christians in his realm. However, soon, he would have bigger and more personal problems to deal with. Shortly after Gregory's imprisonment, Tiridates began to experience a series of extremely strange symptoms. While often perfectly lucid, he would occasionally be overcome with strange fits where he would behave, according to tradition, like a wild boar. It became frighteningly obvious to his subjects that the king was losing his mind. For twelve long years, Gregory languished in Khor Virap, and Tiridates continued to go more and more insane.

It was Tiridates' sister, Khosrovidukht, who turned out to be a lifeline for both Tiridates and his forgotten prisoner. She experienced a vision that only Gregory would be able to cure her brother, and in desperation, she went to Khor Virap to find him. Surprised to discover that he was still alive after twelve years, Khosrovidukht brought Gregory to the raving Tiridates' bedside. Gregory laid his hands on the stricken king and prayed for him to be healed, and the king awoke from his madness, never to have it return again.

So goes Armenian tradition for the reason why Tiridates did what he did next, but history has little doubt of the actions that followed. After he converted to Christianity himself, Tiridates not only stopped persecuting Christians in his domain, but in 301 CE, he also made Christianity the official religion of Armenia. Thus, according to Armenians, it became the first country to officially adopt Christianity as its state religion. And for the next thirteen centuries, the Armenian people would cling to this faith—even though a time would come when it would cost them more dearly than they could have ever expected.

* * * *

As the years passed, the Armenian people continued to prove that they were nothing if not different from everyone else, and they were unafraid to defend their individualism from the rest of the world.

The Sassanid dynasty of the Persian Empire was the next to attempt to overwhelm Armenia in 451 under Yazdegerd II. The Sassanids followed the Zoroastrian religion and unwisely attempted to forcibly convert the Armenians to their religion. The Armenians fought back so strenuously that even the powerful Sassanids were unable to conquer them spiritually, even though they had more success militarily.

For the next two hundred years, Armenia continued to keep its religion stubbornly independent from the encroaching empires—the Persian and the Byzantine Empires—that were attempting to assimilate it. In 634, an Arab invasion resulted in decades of war and then centuries of captivity by the Arabian caliphate of the time. It was only in the late 9th century that Armenia would regain its independence and move forward into the Middle Ages as its own realm, still clinging to Christianity as its state religion. Thus, Armenia supported the European crusaders, proving itself by playing a key role in providing a safe refuge for crusading armies en route to the Holy Land.

When Armenia itself came under attack from Egyptian Mamluks in the 14th century, however, the European powers that had been so quick to use Armenia in its crusades were nowhere to be seen. In fact, for the next several centuries, Armenia would be under constant attack from a variety of Muslim powers. One of these would prove to be Armenia's greatest nemesis and the enemy that would commit the greatest atrocity of them all against the Armenian people: The Ottoman Empire.

# Chapter 2 – The Ottoman Empire

A 19th-century depiction of Mehmed the Conqueror entering Constantinople
*https://commons.wikimedia.org/w/index.php?curid=1818511*

Trampling upon the ashes of the Byzantine Empire rose a new superpower, one that would prove to last for centuries and control much of Europe and Asia: The Ottoman Empire.

The empire was named after its founder, Osman I, a Turkish tribal leader who lived in the late 13th century. Osman was ambitious and ready for more power than simply leading a few tribes in Anatolia, and he and his successors started to carve out a powerful Islamic empire throughout the next two hundred years.

Osman and his successors had little difficulty finding support for their military campaigns. Ever since its rise around the 7th century CE, Islam had spread like wildfire throughout the Middle East, Europe, Asia, and North Africa, and for many Muslims, that meant joining the jihad: an ongoing holy war against all non-Muslims. The jihad was not unlike the crusades, which had been undertaken by the Roman Catholic Church in the Middle Ages. Unlike the ill-fated crusades, however, the jihad would be both enduring and militarily successful, fueled by a belief in its followers that non-Muslims had to be conquered.

With thousands of young people filled with a religious zeal for war, military leaders—who were hungry not just for perceived holiness but also for land and power—were able to amass enormous armies for campaigns all over the world. As the Ottoman Empire grew to engulf Turkey and parts of the Middle East, its greatest rival proved to be the eastern relic of the ancient Roman Empire: The Byzantine Empire. Having been founded on the bedrock of the Eastern Orthodox Church, the Byzantine Empire and Christianity were inextricably linked. That made it a target for the profoundly Islamic Ottoman Empire—and so did its considerable lands and riches, which held tremendous appeal for the rulers of the Ottoman Empire, who were determined to expand their borders and amass power and wealth for their dominion.

The Byzantine Empire, which had been in existence since 330 CE, was in decline by the 15<sup>th</sup> century but nonetheless remained an important power of Christian Europe. Its capital, Constantinople, had long been a jewel of Eastern Europe as a center of power, commerce, government, and culture. And it was Constantinople that the Ottoman rulers—known as sultans—really wanted. To topple Constantinople would be to destroy the Byzantine Empire, and destroying the Byzantine Empire would not only bring huge lands and wealth to the Ottoman Empire, but it would also break down the great wall that stood between the Ottomans and the lushness of Western Europe.

Tamerlane, the terrifying ruler and founder of the Timurid Empire, was the only leader who was able to hold back the Ottoman Empire for long. During the brief and glorious existence of his empire, this Asian conqueror crushed the Ottoman Empire and prevented it from going through his domain to reach the Byzantine Empire. However, Tamerlane's empire would not last long. After his death in 1405, it crumbled to nothing, and the way was clear for the Ottoman Empire to charge through and meet its single greatest foe.

And its sultan, Mehmed II—known to history as Mehmed the Conqueror—was the man for the job.

\* \* \* \*

Mehmed was only twenty years old when he led his army to the very walls of Constantinople, but he was nonetheless an accomplished general.

Mehmed had only been the sultan for two years when he began the siege that would earn him the title of "Mehmed the Conqueror," and he had spent much of that time preparing to besiege Constantinople. Once the greatest city of Eastern Europe, the decline of the Byzantine Empire had robbed the city of the glory it had possessed at its very height, but it was still no small challenge that lay before the young sultan, who was determined to wipe Christianity out of the Byzantine Empire—and, of course, amass those considerable lands for himself. Yet it was still evident that Mehmed had one tremendous advantage: sheer numbers. Constantinople's troops, led by Emperor Constantine XI, numbered only about eight thousand. The Ottomans, on the other hand, came in a great wave of men more than ten times that number.

As was typical of Ottoman sultans, Mehmed invested heavily and focused on warfare, and no siege would be as expensive as that of Constantinople. He built fortresses near the city specifically for the battle and commissioned enormous cannons to be built in order to batter down Constantinople's walls. Outnumbered though the Byzantines were, they had the great advantage of the ancient city's vast defenses. The men inside were few, but their fortress was still one of the most defensible in Europe.

No number of walls or defenses were going to deter Mehmed, however. Cutting off routes for reinforcements to enter the city by either land or sea, he began the siege on April 6th, 1453.

The days that followed, according to historical tradition, were the last 53 days of the Middle Ages. They were long and arduous, not only for the beleaguered Byzantines but also for Mehmed's own men. Viewing many of his own troops as expendable, Mehmed sent them forward in waves upon waves to batter themselves to death against Constantinople's staunch walls. While it was a ruthless choice, it was an effective one; the Ottomans succeeded in systematically breaking down more and more of Constantinople's defenses. Yet somehow, the city clung on, with Emperor Constantine knowing that his city was the last bastion between the Ottomans and the rest of Christendom. For almost two months, the city stood firm against the onslaught.

On the eve of May 26th, Mehmed withdrew his troops. What the Byzantines must have hoped to be a retreat, however, was simply the calm before the storm. Mehmed wasn't giving up—he was preparing for one last great charge, one final bid to bring Constantinople to its knees.

Abandoned by Western European kings, Emperor Constantine's only reinforcements came from a handful of volunteers who had come to Constantinople on their own accord. His repeated pleas for help from the surrounding kings had fallen upon deaf ears. The Byzantine Empire's western counterpart, the Holy Roman Empire, had itself declined in power and was occupied with reformation and struggle within its borders; France and England were decimated after a century of war. No one was coming to Constantine's aid, and he had already lost thousands of his soldiers.

It was with only a handful of men that Constantine waited in the dark city as Mehmed's enormous army, numbering more than 100,000 men, rose in the night like a great bear awakening from its brief hibernation. Mehmed and his men had spent 36 hours in rest and prayer, and now they were ready for the conquest. As midnight approached on May 28th, Mehmed sent forward a batch of cannon fodder: his Christian recruits and poorly equipped infantry. They charged the weakened walls, their aim not to overthrow the enemy but to simply tire the outnumbered Byzantines.

It worked. By the time Mehmed's more seasoned soldiers joined the fray, the Byzantine defenses were buckling. First their general and then their emperor attempted to rally the men but were cut down; panic spread through the troops, with some of them abandoning the battle to rush into the city and protect their families, others fleeing to their ships in a desperate bid to get away. Many, knowing what was coming, knowing that Mehmed would take no prisoners, chose to die on their own terms instead. They climbed the walls of Constantinople, reached the battlements, and flung themselves into the air to be dashed to pieces on the rocks below or swallowed up by the sea.

Those that remained in the city would witness utter devastation. Mehmed had promised to give his soldiers three days of free rein to do as they would with the city they had worked so hard to besiege, and those three days of plundering were almost more horrible than the massive slaughter of May 29th. Women were raped and enslaved, and Ottomans fought with one another over the spoils of war. Any who stood against them were butchered without mercy.

Constantinople had fallen, and the triumphant Mehmed had made his name known as a formidable conqueror. It was not without cost to the Ottomans, however. The Byzantine army had lost half its men; the number of Ottoman casualties is unknown, but according to one eyewitness, it was so vast that the gutters of the city ran scarlet with blood.

Despite the cost, Mehmed had gotten exactly what he wanted. Mehmed made Constantinople the capital of his growing empire, and it remains the capital of Turkey to this day, officially known as Istanbul since 1930. With that, the Byzantine Empire was gone. The time had come for a new and great power, the Ottoman Empire, which would last for hundreds of years. And the fall of Constantinople, gruesome as it was, would not be the bloodiest day in its history.

\* \* \* \*

It was during the 15th century, at the same time as Mehmed and his successors were conquering the Byzantine Empire, that Armenia, too, would fall before the might of the Ottoman Empire, just as many surrounding countries did.

The incorporation of Armenia into the Ottoman Empire was not as sudden and dramatic as the fall of the Byzantine Empire. Instead, it happened slowly and gradually as the prospering Ottomans started to settle in Armenia. As the Ottoman Empire clashed over and over with Persia, Armenia found itself once again to be the battleground of a war in which it had no part, and its people were thrown from one government to the other. By the 15<sup>th</sup> century, actual Armenians comprised only one-quarter of the population of their home country; the Persians were gone, and the Ottoman Empire controlled the whole of Armenia.

The growing Ottoman Empire, although its rulers were devoted Muslims, was not entirely Islamic. Religious minorities, such as Jews and various sects of Christianity, were allowed to exist within its borders. Determined to cling on to the faith they'd held for centuries, the majority of Armenians remained Christian, whether they were Catholic, Orthodox, or even Protestant, as the wake of the Reformation and Renaissance had brought change across the globe. Most Armenians, however, clung to the Orthodox Church, an ancient church founded by two of Jesus' original disciples. Thus, even though Armenians were living right alongside their Turkish counterparts, they remained a very distinct people. They worshiped differently. They spoke a different language. They had different ideals and a whole separate culture, and this made them, in the eyes of the Turks, less than human.

By the late 18<sup>th</sup> century, the Ottoman Empire had started to decline. The brilliance that it had reached in the 16<sup>th</sup> century under the wise rule of Suleiman the Magnificent had started to wear off, and pressure was mounting from the rest of Europe as power shifted and changed around the world. The French Revolution, the Napoleonic Wars, and the end of the Western Holy Roman Empire had made seismic shifts in the power of the world; the Middle East had torn itself from the Ottoman grip, and the once-mighty empire was now struggling to control what was left of its lands.

The decline of Ottoman power was a boon for the Armenians. Their small population was still hanging on and managing to prosper despite oppression from their Turkish government. Still allowed to practice their faith, the Armenians were subject to harsh treatment as being inferior and second-class, and they were known as infidels by the Turks. They were also taxed more harshly than their Muslim neighbors. Nonetheless, the struggling empire was forced to put some reforms into place, and this allowed the Armenians to occupy important positions, even in the government itself.

None of this changed the fact that the Armenians still held on to their religion, their language, and their culture. Their strong national identity never wavered, despite their integration into the Ottoman Empire, and for a time in the mid-18th century, it looked as though they would be allowed to flourish even though they were different.

Nothing could have been further from the truth.

# Chapter 3 – The First Massacres

The struggling Ottoman Empire, already limping and licking its wounds after losing many of its lands, was facing increasing pressure from the rest of the world—and this time, the European powers were not seeking to seize Ottoman lands. Instead, they had taken issue with the very philosophies upon which the Ottoman government was founded.

Ever since the Protestant Reformation in the early 16$^{th}$ century, Europe had been wrestling with the question of religious freedom. Wars broke out all over the continent as Christian powers faced a great rift within their own countries, and it took centuries to move toward tolerance and religious freedom. But by the 18$^{th}$ century, the question had started to settle somewhat. Most countries were at least allowing Protestants to practice in peace, and religious diversity was becoming more common. And it was soon brought to Europe's attention that the Ottoman Empire was late to the party. After the Congress of Berlin finished in July 1878, the subject of the treatment of Armenians by the Ottoman government had become known as the "Armenian question." The rest of Europe was placing increasing pressure on the Ottoman

Empire to reform their treatment of Armenians and other religious and ethnic minorities, and as tensions began to erupt across the continent, the Ottoman Empire pushed back against the pressure.

The Ottoman government's reluctance to treat its minorities better was not solely founded on religion. Instead, Russia—a long-time enemy of the empire—was one of the greatest motivators. Having been a Christian nation for centuries, Russia was not only a military threat but also a religious one. It was feared that Armenians would become more loyal to the Christian government of Russia than the Islamic one of the Ottoman Empire, and considering that there were over one million Armenian people in the empire at the time, this could have been disastrous.

No one feared Russia more than Abdul Hamid II. And his fear and greed would turn out to be a terrible curse for the Armenians because he was their sultan.

* * * *

Abdul Hamid II was born in 1842 to Sultan Abdulmejid, the last in a long line of sultans that had wielded absolute power over their empire. His father enjoyed unrivaled power, and even though Abdul Hamid's mother died when he was a boy, his father—who was a polygamist, like many Ottoman sultans—was still able to provide him with a fairly structured family environment. He was adopted by one of his father's other wives and was able to explore his interests as an adolescent and young man, most notably carpentry and the opera. In fact, Abdul Hamid would be one of the first to translate opera classics into Turkish. In the summer of 1867, when Abdul Hamid was a young man in his twenties, his uncle took him to tour the rest of the world. This was a rare activity for a young prince of the empire, but he was able to accompany his uncle to cities like London and Paris.

After the deposition of Abdul Hamid's older brother, he ascended to the throne in 1876, and many of his subjects thought he would support the rising liberal movement within the empire. It was not only the rest of Europe that was crying out for Ottoman reformation, but also many of its subjects—both minorities and Muslims—wanted change. But Abdul Hamid would do no such thing. When he inherited the empire, it was already on the very brink of disaster. Russia was threatening war, and Abdul Hamid had only been sultan for a year when war was declared.

It lasted only a year. The Ottoman Empire, once the power that had toppled Constantinople, was a shadow of its former self; it stood no chance against the angry behemoth that was Russia (which had also allied with Great Britain). The Congress of Berlin—which made the term "Armenian question" popular in the media—negotiated peace in 1878 after Ottoman defeat.

All across Europe, trouble continued to brew. It became obvious to Abdul Hamid that he would have to find a powerful ally to stand alongside him, and he started to take steps to secure a friendship with Germany. Relations with Russia were still very rocky, especially considering that there was tension between Britain and Germany, and this was only made worse when the Armenians began to look toward their Christian neighbor with longing. In the Ottoman Empire's weakened state, it could not afford to deal with an Armenian rebellion. This could likely have been avoided by providing the Armenians with fairer treatment, but Abdul Hamid was not interested in doing so. He clung to the ways of his forefathers even as the empire they built was crumbling around him.

While the Congress of Berlin had required the Ottoman Empire to reform its policies toward the Armenians, ultimately, Abdul Hamid never complied. Instead, he started to oppress the Armenians even more than before. In response, two Armenian revolutionary parties were formed. Most of the Armenians didn't support these parties, except for a handful of rebels, but they caused widespread panic throughout Abdul Hamid's administration. Abdul Hamid would insult them by calling them cowards and a terrible threat. Even as the ruins of his empire began to fall down around his ears, he refused to see any fault of his own, instead blaming Christian Europe for his troubles and considering the Armenians to be a dangerous group that might "tear out our very guts."

Asked by a journalist about the Armenian question in 1890, Abdul Hamid's words were dark and frightening. "I will soon settle those Armenians."

And in 1894, he attempted to do so. A group of Kurdish brigands had been causing chaos in his empire, and he made no attempt to stop them from wreaking havoc. Instead, he armed them and gave them a focus: they were to make Armenian lives as difficult as possible, and whatever they did, it would be considered legal. These men became known as the Hamidian Regiment, or the *Hamidiye*, and they were quick to exploit the free rein that their sultan had given them. Driving off rural Armenians' livestock, they plundered their homes, raped their women, and butchered those who would dare to stand against them.

The death toll began to rise, and the greater powers of Europe— France, Great Britain, and Russia—decided that something needed to be done. Clearly, the Congress of Berlin had done nothing to curb Abdul Hamid's harsh treatment of the Armenians, and the *Hamidiye* were proof of that. A reform package was sent to him in 1895, demanding that he stop the rampage of his renegade soldiers at once and start implementing the reforms he had promised back in 1878. Abdul Hamid received the package with typical stubbornness. "This business will end in blood," he said darkly.

And it did. Hearing of the reform package, thousands of Armenians gathered in Constantinople to show their support of the reforms and demanded that they be implemented. For some of them, October 1ˢᵗ, 1895, would be their last day. When the rally began to get loud and angry as the people petitioned for a better life, Turkish policemen were sent in to break it up. Instead of bringing help to the Armenians, the reforms had already brought nothing but even more violence.

It was nothing compared to the atrocities that would follow.

* * * *

Susan Wheeler had come to the Ottoman Empire to minister to a people oppressed by hatred. She hadn't expected to flee for her life.

The Armenian question was a European concern, but it was a topic that spread like wildfire throughout the United States. Children were told to finish their dinner no longer because of the "starving children in Africa," but because of the "starving children in Armenia." Armenians became the cause of the day, and many wealthy Americans donated to the Red Cross and other organizations that were trying to help the people there. Yet for some Americans, simply raising awareness or funds was simply not enough. Some of them felt convicted to go to Armenia themselves, and Susan and her husband, Reverend Crosby Howard Wheeler, were among them.

In their book "A Bouquet from Our Missionary Garden," Susan and Crosby would tell the story of how they traveled to Harput, Turkey, in order to support the Armenian Christians in their persecution, decades before the massacres started. They set up a mission station to provide a place of worship as well as schools for Christian children, and as news of massacres in Constantinople and other areas of Turkey began to reach them, they knew that trouble was coming. But like many Protestant American missionaries, the Wheelers refused to flee back to a home country where there was both peace and freedom. Instead, they held firm and waited for the *Hamidiye* to descend upon Harput.

The officials in the city had promised to protect the Armenians from the *Hamidiye*, and when the first of the frightening Kurds began to seep out of the mountains—the regiment streaming down onto the plain like rivers of blood—Harput's cannons were made ready to fire. Terrified, Armenians poured into the mission station, desperate for refuge; none were turned away, although Crosby, at this point, was wheelchair-bound. Susan and her helpers watched and prayed as the *Hamidiye* swept toward the city while the cannons were being loaded. The city would protect them. The city had said it would.

The city had lied. When the great crack of the cannon rang through the air and the smell of gunpowder unleashed battle on the senses, the ammunition was not launched toward the marauding *Hamidiye*. Instead, the cannons were firing on the Armenian quarter of the city itself. The Harput defenses would not be doing any defending against the *Hamidiye*—instead, Susan had to watch, appalled, as the Armenians' own home city was turned against them. Death rained down upon their homes, and when the *Hamidiye* burst into the city itself, matters were made much worse. They were bent not only on massacring the people but also on destroying their homes.

Susan and her companions fled from one missionary building to the other, pausing to stare out of the windows as flames sprang up throughout the city in the falling darkness. Smoke rose above Harput, leaving the Muslim Turks' homes untouched; the Armenians were the target, and they would be shown no mercy. Fearing for their lives, Armenians and missionaries alike were forced to flee the schools and churches where they were seeking refuge, heading for the newest building that the Wheelers had worked tirelessly to erect. It was the library, but getting there would not be easy. Susan was aging herself; Crosby would have to be carried, and in the utter pandemonium, she had no idea how this could be done.

Crosby's salvation came from an unlikely quarter: a group of Kurdish people, just like the *Hamidiye*. But while these young men shared the same ethnicity with the murderers plundering the city, they had been Crosby's students, and they refused to join their kinfolk's rampage. Instead, they scooped Crosby into a rocking chair and carried him to the library, hundreds of missionaries and Armenians hot on their heels.

Hidden away in the library, defended by a few brave volunteers in a fire engine, Susan, Crosby, and their friends watched as the Christian part of the city burned around them. Men, women, and children were butchered by the *Hamidiye* or succumbed to the blaze.

The total casualties in Harput throughout the killings of 1894 to 1896—a spate of awful violence that became known as the Hamidian massacres—numbered about 40,000. And Harput was not the only region of the empire to suffer. All across the Ottoman Empire, Armenians were killed in cold blood. Eyewitnesses described piles of corpses, looted for their clothing and horribly mutilated postmortem, killed without regard for age or gender. They were shot, burned, drowned, and thrown into mass graves. Families were robbed of their breadwinners and starved slowly as their neighbors walked in peace thanks to a difference in race and religion. On one terrible night, 3,000 Armenians perished when the cathedral they were hiding in was burned to the ground.

The handful of Armenian revolutionaries attempted to fight back, but their efforts were to no avail. In fact, Abdul Hamid only brought an end to the violence when all of the revolutionaries had been driven out of the empire or killed. Despite pleas for international aid, no white knight would come riding to the aid of the Armenians. Even the missionaries, who came from Great Britain, America, and other countries, could do little other than to assist the survivors of the violence, people who had been left without homes, food, or families. The killing only stopped because Abdul Hamid had decided that the answer to the Armenian question had been written on the pages of history with the blood of the people.

The Hamidian massacres ended in 1896, with a death toll estimated to be as high as 300,000 people—more than one-quarter of the Armenian population of the Ottoman Empire at the time. When the violence was over, the Armenian people were left decimated, not only by the killings but also by the fact that the *Hamidiye* had forced hundreds of villages to convert to Islam or die. And while many Armenians did convert in the face of death, others refused to recant their faith. Even after the massacres, the Armenian populace in general still stubbornly held on to the Christian religion that had given them their cultural identity.

In 1905, almost ten years after the end of the massacres, Armenian revolutionaries had regrouped and attempted to assassinate Abdul Hamid, the man behind hundreds of thousands of deaths. They rigged a car with explosives and timed it to explode at the moment when Abdul Hamid normally left his favorite mosque after Friday prayers. But the attempt was ill-fated. Abdul Hamid happened to come across a friend in the mosque and spent some time talking with him, failing to come out at his usual time. The car did explode, and it took the lives of 26 people with it. But Abdul Hamid was not one of those people.

Nonetheless, his rule would not last much longer. Military coups and an unconstitutional government peppered the last few years of his reign. The time of the sultans was coming to an end. A revolution was coming—this time, though, not from bitter Armenians but from the Turkish people themselves.

# Chapter 4 – The Young Turk Revolution

"For yourselves know perfectly that the day of the Lord so cometh as a thief in the night. For when they shall say, Peace and safety; then sudden destruction cometh upon them, as travail upon a woman with child; and they shall not escape."

So wrote the apostle Paul, almost 2,000 years before the Young Turk Revolution, in a letter addressed to the budding Christian church in a city then known as Thessalonica. Then a part of Greece, Thessalonica was captured by the Ottoman Empire in the 15ᵗʰ century and had since become known as Salonika—and also as one of the most tolerant and culturally diverse cities in Europe.

It was ironic that Salonika was part of the Ottoman Empire, considering that the empire was one of the worst places in the world to be a religious or ethnic minority. Yet it was a strange little oasis of freedom and tolerance in the great desert of hatred that the empire had become under the reign of Abdul Hamid. In its streets, Jews and Turks, Muslims and Albanians, Armenians and Arabs were able to rub shoulders without fear of as much persecution as their fellows were suffering in the rest of the empire. And it was in Salonika that a revolution would be born—one that began with pure and just ideals but ended in genocide.

* * * *

The Young Turk Revolution occurred in 1908 in the Ottoman Empire, but its roots went as far back as Paris, 1799. The French Revolution was one of the greatest influences on the revolution that the Young Turks were planning, and many of the revolutionary leaders themselves planned their moves while they were in exile in Paris and other Western European cities.

Ever since 1878, Abdul Hamid had been ruling over the Ottoman Empire without a constitution, having suspended Parliament. His reasons for suspending the Turkish constitution were far-fetched; he claimed that democracy was not going to work until the masses had been educated, and the constitution would be reinstated once the majority of the Ottoman populace was more educated. Of course, Abdul Hamid made no attempts whatsoever to further education in his empire, and for thirty years, he simply did whatever he wanted, unbound by any constitutional laws. He was, by definition, an autocratic tyrant, and his massacre of the Armenians had made him even less popular with many of his citizens as well as the rest of Europe, who had dubbed him "the Red Sultan" for his bloody actions.

His unconstitutional government had long been chafing at his subjects, and not just with the Armenians. Powerful Turks within his administration were also looking for something different, and prominent among these were the Young Turks, a group of forward-thinking military officers. Together with several other groups that wished to promote progress in the empire, the Young Turks formed the Community of Union and Progress (CUP), a political party bent on revolution to topple the absolute monarchy once and for all.

Several smaller parties had come together to form the CUP, and one of them was the Armenian Revolutionary Federation (ARF), led by Khachatur Maloumian. The ARF had been responsible for many of the rebel activities around the same time as the Hamidian massacres, and it would have been understandable if Maloumian had viewed the Young Turks with suspicion. But at the Second Congress of the Ottoman Opposition, which was held in 1907 in Paris, the Young Turks spoke of something intoxicating and glorious, something that all Armenians desperately needed: justice. The Young Turks' vision was one of liberty, equality, justice, and freedom, one where every citizen of the empire— regardless of race or religion—would be allowed to stand on equal footing with his peers. If the Young Turks succeeded, there would be no more excessive taxation of Christian groups like the Armenians. There would be no more discrimination, oppression, or massacres. Backed by Armenian supporters, Maloumian allied his party with the CUP, and together with the Young Turks, they began to plan a revolution.

Basing many of their operations in Salonika, the Young Turks started to plan a way to bring back the constitution and get Parliament back into session. The army would be crucial to their plans. Paranoid as he was, Abdul Hamid had known for years that some of his military officers were discontent with him, so he responded by cutting the army's funding significantly, leaving the empire defenseless as other power-hungry European countries started to prey on its borders, including France, Russia, Great Britain, and Austria-Hungary. This fueled even more discontent among the military officers for whom the defense of the empire was a matter of professional pride. Once the finest military in Europe, the Ottoman Empire's army had become a joke, and its officers were not amused.

It was two of its adjutant-majors, Ismail Enver Pasha and Ahmed Niyazi—Enver Pasha was Turkish, Niyazi was Albanian—who sparked the revolt. Niyazi was the first to act on July 3rd, 1908. Abdul Hamid suspected that his loyalties did not lie with the sultan and had him investigated, and Niyazi responded by raiding the military base he commanded and then fleeing into the mountains with 200 of his followers. Enver Pasha was quick to follow, and so were many other military officers. They regrouped and then started to move on Constantinople. When Abdul Hamid tried to get the remainder of his army to go out and fight them, they refused. The sultan realized, suddenly and terribly, how defenseless he really was if his own army would not fight for him.

Three days after Niyazi's raid, the CUP issued a revolutionary proclamation. They wanted the constitution and Parliament back, and if Abdul Hamid did not comply, there would be war. Beaten, the sultan had no choice. On July 24th, he brought back Parliament, and the absolute monarchy of the Ottoman Empire was at an end.

It was a day of absolute rejoicing for the minorities of the Ottoman Empire. The celebrations turned into a loud and colorful party in the streets of Constantinople as citizens of the empire celebrated by wearing red and white, the colors of the empire's flag. Albanian and Armenian, Jewish and Greek, Turk and Arab—they all took to the streets as equals, and for one glorious day, they were united under the common title of being human.

If they had known what was coming, they would not have danced. They would have hidden.

* * * *

Adana burned and not only with fire.

Smoke towered above the city, black and thick and choking, as the scarlet flames licked around the homes of innocent families and reduced them to ashes. The streets were filled with screams, and they echoed the appearance of the fire, as blazing hatred and choking terror roared from one city block to the other. Shouts of rage, screams of pain, running feet, total anarchy—the once-prosperous city was reduced to a battleground, and the fight was cruelly unbalanced.

Elizabeth S. Webb was in the very same shoes in which Susan Wheeler had walked a path of terror and blood fourteen years earlier. Like Susan, she was an American Protestant missionary who had come to Adana to help the Christians, although their situation up until a few months ago had not been anywhere near as desperate as the predicament of the Armenians in Harput had been in Susan's time. Elizabeth had thought that she'd come to help the Armenians build better lives in a better time. Now, with horror, she was forced to witness the selfsame violence that Susan had endured in Harput.

Elizabeth was one of the foreign eyewitnesses who wrote vivid testimonies about the terrible violence that occurred in Adana in April of 1909. While the Armenians suffered far more than the American missionaries, they were not free to go home to a country that would hear them and publish detailed accounts of what had truly happened. And so, we turn to the words of these missionaries to paint a picture of the devastation that took place in Adana.

It had all started with a counter-coup. After the Young Turks succeeded in reinstating Parliament (the CUP even managed to get some seats in it), religious minorities in the country had been overjoyed to hear that they planned to abandon Abdul Hamid's policies of governing strictly in line with Islam. In fact, the CUP would stay out of religion entirely; it wished to build a secular government and allow its subjects to worship however they wanted. This caused a massive public outcry, especially from the Muslim community. When Christians were authorized to bear arms for the first time in centuries, panic began to spread. It was less than twenty years after the Hamidian massacres, after all. Would the Armenians take their revenge? Bitter and resentful, many Armenian and other Christian preachers made matters worse, pouring fuel on the fire by encouraging their members to arm themselves. A small and angry handful even abandoned the doctrine of their own churches and started to encourage the Armenians to take revenge.

Petrified, Abdul Hamid's loyalists gathered support from frightened Muslims and launched a counter-coup on April 13th, 1909. The coup was successful; the Young Turks were ousted, and for ten days of terror, Abdul Hamid reigned once more with absolute power. His message was clear. The Christians were a threat, and the Armenians needed to be exterminated.

Empowered by their taste of freedom, the Armenians refused to take this lying down. When news of the coup reached the city of Adana on April 14th, they started an angry and violent riot. The Muslim population was scared to death, believing that the Armenians were finally coming to take revenge. But the riot was nothing more than a disorganized and angry expression of a nation's fear and frustration. There was no leader of the riot, no unifying Armenian commander who could amass his people into a real threat to the Muslims. Fear and hatred, however, knows no reason. The Muslim population rose up, formed a furious mob, and fell upon the Armenians without mercy.

The violence that blossomed through Adana and its surroundings claimed almost 2,000 Turkish lives, according to the official Ottoman figures. Those same figures claim that about 5,000 Armenians were killed and that there was no massacre, simply a battle as the Turks attempted to defend themselves from marauding Armenians. Foreign witnesses, however, tell a very different story. Armenians began to flee to British and French embassies as the massacres raged on, desperate for help, and this time, Europe would not stand by and watch the slaughter. Warships were sent to pacify the situation, and courageous consulates headed out onto the streets themselves in a bid to prevent the Hamidian massacres from happening all over again.

They were only partially successful. By the end of April, the Young Turks had managed to wrest back the government and formally deposed Abdul Hamid. But the Red Sultan's swansong had cost the lives of between 20,000 and 30,000 Armenians.

Elizabeth S. Webb's account remains one of the most terrifying and vivid. She tells of how one of her American companions, clutching the hand of an Armenian preacher, tried to flee across an empty street to the safety of a mission building. The two men were in the middle of the street when an angry mob came charging toward them, armed with knives and guns. Knowing what was coming, the American seized his Armenian friend and pulled him into his arms, trying to shield him with his body. He screamed at the injustice of it, screamed that the Armenian was unarmed and harmless. There was no way that he could have hurt them, even if he wanted to. But despite the American's best efforts, the mob would have none of it. They killed him where he stood and went on with their rampage as the heartbroken American dragged his friend's dead body to safety.

To this very day, the government of Turkey denies that the Adana massacre ever happened, despite the fact that due to the many casualties three orphanages had to be built in Adana and its surroundings just to accommodate the children who had lost their parents in the violence. The Grand Vizier, Hüseyin Hilmi Pasha, went so far as to say with utter confidence that "there will never be another massacre."

He could not have been more wrong. The Hamidian and Adana massacres were just a taste of the appalling events that were to come.

# Chapter 5 – The World Goes to War

The Young Turks had managed to claw back the power they had briefly lost during the counter-coup of 1909, leading many Armenians and other religious minorities to breathe a sigh of relief. Perhaps Abdul Hamid's brief and terrible return to power had been nothing more than the death throes of the old days. After all, the Young Turks had said that they would make things better.

The Young Turks did not make things better. In fact, they made them worse. The CUP deposed Abdul Hamid and put his brother, Sultan Mehmed V, on the throne; however, it was obvious that Mehmed was little more than a figurehead. The real power lay in the hands of the CUP, and it was immediately faced with a difficult new question: whether it was more important to achieve its vision of an ethnically diverse multi-national state or to keep the borders of the Ottoman Empire from further disintegrating. Every prominent power in Europe was looking for a piece of the empire, and its leaders felt besieged on every side.

Faced with the threat of invasion and of losing what remained of the Ottoman Empire, the new government began to descend into corruption. The CUP turned out not to be the savior that Turkey's people sought, and things came to a head when the new government was forced to decide what would be its greatest priority: promoting the peaceful coexistence of a diverse and varied people within the empire or avoiding the loss of imperial lands to the rest of the world. History might have turned out very differently if the CUP had chosen to emphasize the former at the cost of losing some of its lands and power. Instead, it was decided that it would be more important to present a united front and avoid the further loss of lands to the predatory powers of the rest of Europe, and so, the CUP attempted to unite the Ottoman Empire under one singular identity: that of being Turkish.

It might have worked if everyone in the Ottoman Empire really was Turkish. But they weren't; while Turks made up the majority of the population, there were also Armenians, Arabs, Albanians, Jews, Greeks, other minorities who did not identify as being Turkish. They spoke a different language, worshiped a different god, and had an entirely separate culture and identity. For the Armenians, who had clung so stubbornly to their ways even in the face of massacres and who had been hoping so desperately for change under the Young Turk regime, it was a terrible blow to be told that they now had to be Turkish.

Turkification, as the CUP's new policy became known, was an old idea, dating back to the end of the $19^{th}$ century as part of the Ottoman Empire's bid for unification. It was the Young Turks, however, who really brought Turkification into full force in the 1910s. Turkification was an attempt to wholly assimilate the minorities within the empire, transforming all of the peoples into Turks.

The leaders of the CUP at the time, who were the real rulers of the Ottoman Empire as the sultans had been reduced to little more than figureheads, were a triumvirate of powerful officials in the government. Mehmed Talaat Pasha was the Grand Vizier; Ismail Enver Pasha, who had been one of the first military commanders involved in the Young Turk Revolution, was the Minister of War; and Ahmed Djemal Pasha was the Minister of the Navy. They would go down in history as the "Three Pashas," and all three of them firmly believed that Turkification would lead to power and unity for the Ottoman Empire and thus security for its people as well as power for themselves. If thousands of people had to give up their way of living and their faith, then it would be a necessary sacrifice to secure their safety.

They could not have been more wrong. Instead of uniting the citizens of the empire under one uniform culture, Turkification created tremendous rifts between the Turks and the minorities who had just started on the road to reconciliation. Brainwashed by government propaganda that all non-Turks were inferior and dangerous, Turks once more found themselves viewing minorities—not just Armenians—with deep suspicion. Enraged by the fact that they had effectively been told to abandon their own culture, many Armenians responded by refusing to become Turkified at all. They also refused to convert to Islam.

While outright persecution did not begin immediately, Armenians certainly felt the pinch of Turkification very early on. They were still being taxed more harshly than their Muslim counterparts and were denied many of the privileges that their fellow citizens were enjoying by virtue of simply being Turkish. Worse, the official language used in courts and other government institutions throughout the Ottoman Empire had been changed to Turkish, which many Armenians and other minorities did not speak. The Three Pashas had tried to assimilate the minorities of the empire; instead, they had succeeded in alienating them even further.

The First Balkan War was evidence of how badly Turkification was failing to create unity. Tired of oppression and disappointed that the Young Turks had failed to deliver everything that they had promised, a group of ethnic minorities living in the Ottoman Empire appealed to their native countries for help. In response, Greece, Serbia, Bulgaria, and Montenegro—all newly independent from the empire but all with ethnic populations still residing alongside the Ottomans—joined forces against the Turks. Known as the Balkan League, these allies declared war on the Turks in 1912, and they fought a brutal and bloody war against them. The war was ugly but also short-lived; by the end of the year, the Ottoman Empire had lost most of its vast European territories to the Balkan League. Instead of reforming their policies toward minorities, however, the Three Pashas saw the First Balkan War as being symptomatic of the problem of having non-Turks within the empire. Turkification was forced harder and harder on the minorities.

As discontent spread like a disease through the empire, it would soon face much bigger problems. For the first time in history, the entire world was about to go to war.

\* \* \* \*

The Europe of 1914 was tinder, drenched in lighter fluid. All it would take was a single spark to set the whole continent—and, with it, the rest of the world—alight. And that spark would find its origins in the Second Balkan War.

After winning many territories back from the Ottoman Empire, the members of the Balkan League almost immediately started fighting among themselves over how to split the spoils of the war. The territories that the victors had gained were considerable, and it caused a profound rift between the members of the League. By 1913, Greece and Serbia had formed an alliance against Bulgaria. In retaliation, Bulgaria turned to its powerful neighbor, Austria, for help. Austria was not an inconsiderable power at the time, and Greece and Serbia saw this as a significant threat. They declared war on Bulgaria in the summer of 1913.

The Second Balkan War, like its predecessor, was as savage as it was short-lived. In only two months, Bulgaria—despite its mighty ally—had been brought to its knees. Greece and Serbia got what they wanted, but it was still clear that Bulgaria and Austria together were a threat to the countries that were just starting to recover from centuries of Ottoman rule.

The rest of Europe was similarly embroiled in simmering conflicts. Complicated alliances patterned Europe and Asia: Serbia was in alliance with Russia, which was allied with France, which was an ally of Great Britain, which in turn was allied with Japan. Any move from a single country could trigger a snowball effect of wars with other countries as they moved to defend their allies. The Ottoman Empire, for its part, was not officially allied with anyone in this way but retained its good relationship with Germany, knowing that trouble was coming.

Tensions over imperial lands in Africa and Asia contributed to an arms race between the countries as each tried to prove to the other that it was too powerful to attack. As a result, by 1914, the whole of Europe was armed to the teeth and spoiling for a fight. All it needed was a reason, and a Serbian man named Gavrilo Princip would provide the reason for a war that would claim almost seventeen million lives.

Princip was a Serbian nationalist. While Serbia had fought against Austria in the Second Balkan War, there were still Serbs and other Slavic peoples living in Austria at the time, and they desired freedom from Austria's imperialistic ideals, which dated back to its glory days as the seat of the Habsburg rulers of the Holy Roman Empire centuries before. It was a Serbian terrorist group, known as the Black Hand, that would eventually decide to do something less than diplomatic about this problem. And Princip was the trigger finger of the Black Hand—a fact that he proved when he assassinated Austrian heir apparent Archduke Franz Ferdinand and his wife, Sophie, on June 28th, 1914.

At once, the whole of Europe was in a total uproar. Austria was determined to open war on Serbia, but it was forced to hesitate because of Serbia's powerful ally Russia, which had even more powerful allies of its own. Austria, however, was backed by the German Kaiser Wilhelm II. Bolstered by the knowledge of its own strong ally, Austria-Hungary gave Serbia an impossible ultimatum. The ultimatum, which demanded that Serbia should allow their enemies to investigate the assassination in Serbia, had been drafted with the knowledge that it could not possibly have been accepted. It was not so much a way out of the war as a way to shift the blame for it. Serbia, left without a choice, responded by declaring war. Within days, Austria-Hungary and Germany found themselves facing a conflict not only with Serbia but also with Russia and its allies, Great Britain, France, and Belgium.

August 4th, 1914, marked the beginning of the war. Germany spearheaded an invasion into France while at the same time launching an attack on Russia in the east. The effect on France was utterly devastating as brilliant German commanders devastated the country, taking the city of Liège by August 15th.

For several months, the Ottoman Empire, which was not directly involved in the conflict, sat back and watched as Europe burned. And the Three Pashas had a good reason for not wanting to get involved in what was blossoming into the First World War. Decades of war and revolution had left the Ottoman Empire depleted and exhausted, and as the fragile Young Turk movement struggled to pick up the pieces after the devastating First Balkan War, it appeared that engaging in the First World War would be disastrous. However, as Germany began to amass victory after victory, Enver Pasha started to reconsider. Joining the war on the German side could be a blessing for the Ottoman Empire if it ended in victory. It could be the Hail Mary that the empire needed to solidify its rapidly crumbling borders—a last bid to gain back its old power.

Despite opposition from the prime minister, Enver Pasha quickly gained the support of the other two Pashas, and the Ottoman Empire entered World War I on October 28th, 1914, fighting alongside Germany.

Most of the fighting in which the Ottomans became involved would occur in the Middle East and the Balkans, not directly within the empire's borders. Dismayed, its citizens would still be forced to witness, after having endured massacres and a revolution, a new evil: a world war. What could possibly be worse?

They would soon find out the answer to that question.

# Chapter 6 – Red Sunday

Soghomon Soghomonian had probably first heard the words of "Dle Yaman" on the flanks of Mount Ararat when he was a freshly orphaned preteen. Back in the 1880s, it was a love song, and the passionate edge of its lyrics blew across the mountain breeze to light something in young Soghomon's heart. The song was desperate and whimsical and lovesick.

*Alas! Alas! Our homes face each other,*

*Oh, alas! Isn't it enough that my eyes send you a sign?*

*Alas! Alas! Oh my love!*

*Oh, alas! Isn't it enough that my eyes send you a sign?*

Little did Soghomon know that "Dle Yaman" would one day be so much more than a folksy old love song, especially to him. It would become a song of loss, a loss so deep and palpable that the whole world felt the brunt of its agony.

* * * *

Soghomon Soghomonian, born a Christian Armenian in 1869, is better known by his ordained name of Komitas. Not only was he a leader in the Armenian Church, but he also grew up to become a singer and composer who would single-handedly build the foundation for Armenian folk music as it is known today. And like 235 fellow Armenians, Komitas was deported on the day the Armenian Genocide began: April 24th, 1915.

Ever since the Ottoman Empire had joined World War I, life had gotten progressively harder for the Armenians, particularly because the Islamic religious authorities took the opportunity to declare war too. Their war, however, would not be against the enemies of Germany. It would be a holy war, a jihad against all non-Christians (except for their allies in World War I, conveniently). This meant that even the Armenian citizens within the Ottoman Empire itself would not be spared. The hope that the revolution of 1908 had brought was now soundly snuffed out as another wave of oppression crushed the Armenians. Muslims viewed them as a target, and even secular leaders viewed them with suspicion and even fear. Since the Ottomans had spent decades making life unbearable for all Armenian people, it would be no surprise if the Armenians decided to betray the Ottoman Empire in favor of neighboring Russia. To this end, the government launched a campaign to remove all weapons from Armenian possession. The people were stripped of anything that could be used for either revolt or self-defense, down to their very kitchen knives.

Some of the Armenians certainly were ready to ally with Russia, hoping that their lives would be a little better in a Christian country. The majority, however, simply attempted to continue with their daily lives as well as they could in the face of a world war. They were just ordinary people doing ordinary things. They posed little threat, but Enver Pasha would not be persuaded to believe this.

This became evident when Enver Pasha took his army to Sarikamish, Russia. He planned to claim back some of the lands that the Ottomans had lost to Russia in the Russo-Turkish War in the 1870s, but it was an ambitious plan doomed to fail, and Enver Pasha's army was all but destroyed by Russian troops. Enraged, Enver Pasha blamed the Armenians in the area, saying that they had sided with the Russians and caused the loss of countless Turkish lives. This was not entirely untrue; it was accurate that some Armenian volunteers had joined the Russian tsar's forces, but their numbers and forces were not to blame for the defeat. Instead, it was more likely due to Enver Pasha's incompetence.

Nonetheless, panic about perceived dangers from Armenians, fueled by propaganda, spread throughout the Ottoman army, and the Armenian men who had been drafted into the army were removed from passive duty, stripped of their arms, and transferred to so-called labor battalions to do the boring, laborious work of warfare. Thus, Enver Pasha attempted to ensure that every Armenian in the empire was disarmed.

By April 1915, tensions were skyrocketing throughout the Ottoman Empire. While some Armenians had joined forces with the Russians, the vast majority of them were terrified and helpless within the empire—and for good reason. Violent gangs of criminals began to form with one intent: to kill the Armenians. And the Turkish police did little to stop them as chaos blossomed across the empire, with Armenians being driven out of their homes and butchered in the streets by the gangs.

The violence was particularly harsh in the area of Van, an Ottoman city near the Russian border. Armenians in the towns and villages surrounding Van found themselves at war with the gangs that sought to murder them all; the police were no help whatsoever, and the Armenians had been deprived of any means to defend themselves from their marauding enemies. Desperate, thousands of Armenians fled to the city itself. Despite being grossly outnumbered by the Turks, the Armenians engaged in a bloody and disorganized hand-to-hand battle in the streets of Van. Thousands perished, but eventually, they managed to gain control over the city. Keeping the gates open for refugees, who streamed in from the surrounding countryside in vast numbers, the Armenians prayed that Van would prove to be a safe refuge. Yet with only 1,500 men to defend it (armed with about 1,000 pistols and 300 rifles, which was fewer guns than men), the situation remained appallingly grim.

It would soon become grimmer still. On April 19th, 1915, a military commander named Jevdet Bey commanded the city to surrender 4,000 conscripts for the labor battalions. His command was a poor pretense; the Armenians were well aware that if they sent him those men, they would be promptly executed. Trying to buy some time, they offered to send him 500 men and some exemption money instead. But Jevdet refused. He never wanted soldiers; he wanted blood, and he would get it. Calling the Armenians rebellious (which they certainly were, but they were facing mass persecution), Jevdet angrily claimed that he was going to kill "every Christian man, woman and child" in the city.

If peaceful surrender had been an option, it is possible the Armenians might have taken it. The odds were terrible; Jevdet had at his command about 5,000 seasoned soldiers, and Enver Pasha's 1st Expeditionary Force—numbering around 60,000—was nearby. The Armenians must have known that to fight back would mean they would die, but at least they would die fighting instead of being brutally executed in cold blood.

Things came to a head on April 20th, 1915. A lone woman—bruised, battered, exhausted, and traumatized beyond all expression—came stumbling across the ravaged countryside, heading for the oasis of peace that she hoped Van would be. She had survived so much, and she was utterly desperate, desperate enough that in her panicking flight toward the city, she strayed too close to the Ottoman soldiers. They seized her, and their intentions were clear as they pawed at her body and pushed her around. Unable to watch, a pair of Armenian men burst out of Van and rushed to her aid. Their effort was as pathetic as it was courageous. They were promptly shot, one after the other, and Jevdet saw this as the perfect excuse to attack. He sent his soldiers forward, and the siege of Van, which is often referred to as the Defense of Van, began.

Hopelessly outnumbered though they were, the Armenians succeeded in keeping the city gates open to the rivers of refugees that continued to pour into the city; at this point, there were about 45,000 vulnerable innocents inside the city, defended by a mere courageous handful. Despite the best efforts of their shoestring guard, thousands of the refugees were butchered.

Still, the Ottoman government had not yet actually made it legal to kill Armenians. But all that would change on April 24th, 1915. The Defense of Van was still raging when, 785 miles away, an official act of ruthless persecution against ethnic Armenians would take place in the very capital of the Ottoman Empire.

Constantinople was not the jewel of culture and commerce that it had been in the era of the Byzantine Empire, but it was nonetheless a center of academia and art in the Ottoman Empire. Despite the disadvantages imposed upon them by their race, many Armenians had managed to make names for themselves as important intellectuals within the city. Soghomon Soghomonian, by this time known as Father Komitas, was one of them. Having spent years traveling the world and performing Armenian folk music, Komitas had become something of a celebrity. It would perhaps have been wiser for him to stay in Europe, where most people were sympathetic to the Armenian cause and saw him as a tragic but wonderful artist; instead, he had come home to Constantinople.

Like hundreds of other Armenian intellectuals, Komitas was peacefully passing the evening of April 23rd, 1915, when the Ottomans came. Storming into homes and workplaces, Turkish soldiers and police arrested a total of about 235 Armenian intellectuals that night. They no longer had the right to be citizens of the Ottoman Empire, they were told. They would be briefly held in cells in Constantinople before being deported to the Syrian Desert.

Over the next few days, thousands more Armenians were rounded up and forced out of the city. In the meantime, Van continued to stand against Jevdet's angry horde; in fact, the siege would continue until May 17th when Russian relief forces would finally come to the rescue. It was still too late for about 50,000 Armenians, some of them soldiers but many of them petrified refugees that had fled to the city. Those who survived maintained control of the city with the help of the Russians.

By that time, thousands more Armenians were being forced to leave the empire that had been so cruel to them yet was the only home their people had known for thousands of years. While many of the intellectuals arrested on April 24th were executed, Komitas survived, but only as a shadow of his former self. The events of the deportation—and, along the way, the rape and execution of hundreds of Armenians—would leave a scar on his mind that never could heal.

Nobody could blame him, for what Komitas and others had to endure was nothing short of a death march.

# Chapter 7 – Death March

**Refugees in a Syrian camp**
*https://commons.wikimedia.org/w/index.php?curid=9462125*

Considering that Armin T. Wegner was a member of the German army, it was a little surprising that he chose to become one of the Armenians' greatest allies.

When war broke out in 1914, Wegner—then 28 years old—could not face the idea of taking up arms expressly to kill others. He had to join the army, however, and he did so as a combat medic. Always driven by a strongly altruistic desire to make the world a better place, Wegner had little taste for war itself, but he certainly had no lack of courage. Shortly after being sent to the Middle Eastern front, he earned an Iron Cross for his bravery in helping wounded soldiers under heavy fire.

But Wegner hadn't just come to help the wounded. He'd come to document the events of the war—and he had long been suspicious that the Ottoman Empire's policy against Armenians was not the act of defense that its leadership claimed. The leaders of the Ottoman Empire had protested that deporting all of the Armenians was its only choice in order to protect itself from rebellious alliances between Armenians and Russians. Wegner had a hunch that this wasn't true. But what he would witness was far worse than anything he could have ever imagined.

The arrest of several thousand Armenians in Constantinople in April 1915 was only the beginning of the deportations. The Ottoman government wanted them gone, and they would march those Armenians across the brutal Syrian Desert in the growing heat of summer and then dump them in the small town of Deir ez-Zor in Syria. The town could not possibly accommodate the masses of Armenians that were flooding in, but the Ottomans were not concerned with this. All of the Armenians could perish in that desert for all they cared.

And those masses of Armenians were truly massive. When Talaat and the other two Pashas first ordered the deportation of Armenians, it was supposed to include only those who had been involved in the violence in Van and other areas of the Ottoman Empire (violence which, ironically, Talaat referred to as "massacres"). By May 29th, 1915, a new law had been passed. This Tehcir Law was the death knell for hundreds of thousands of Armenian people.

The Tehcir Law allowed Ottoman officials to summarily deport, without any form of trial or investigation and at their discretion, any Armenian person that was viewed to be a threat to national security. Of course, for many officials, there was no need to sense a threat at all. Simply being Armenian was reason enough for thousands of innocent people to be arrested, and once they were arrested, they were sent to the Syrian Desert to die.

Many did not even make it that far. The forced removal of the Armenians from the Ottoman Empire was utterly brutal. Coming from the cool green mountainsides of Anatolia, the Armenians were forced to make their way, generally on foot, across the stark landscape of the desert.

All of them suffered; relief was offered only in a tiny degree to the very rich, who were able to pay off guards to give them more food. But one has to let one's heart wander to those who were only children when the genocide began. To follow the journey of an Armenian child along one of those death marches is almost incomprehensible; the suffering that all of those people endured (or failed to endure) is almost too hard to imagine. But for the sake of the fallen, let us attempt to imagine it. Let us attempt to imagine what it would be like to be an Armenian child dragged from a rural home in the green foothills where your ancestors had lived long before the Ottoman Empire even had a name.

Roughly arrested by police, military, or ordinary Turkish citizens (who were, in many cases, given free rein to "assist" the military in the arrest and persecution of Armenians), you and your family would possibly be held in some dank and overcrowded cell for a brief time while other people like you were rounded up. Did the children ask questions? Did they want their parents to tell them why these scary men were dragging them away? Did they ask what they'd done wrong? Did they see their own mothers and fathers cry? Or was it worse than that—

were they stripped away from their families and carried off by brutal strangers into the night?

If you were a woman or even a comely enough young girl, your lot was even unhappier than that of your male counterparts. Fueled by uncontrolled rage and desire, having left their own wives or girlfriends behind to join the army, the soldiers were savage in their treatment of the women and girls. Mothers were raped in front of their children, brides in front of their grooms. Sometimes repeatedly, their bodies were violated over and over by multiple men until they were left to die by the wayside or perhaps stripped naked and sold into slavery in one of the cities.

Stripped of dignity, stripped of the innocence of childhood, stripped perhaps of your mother or sisters or your own rights to your body, you would then be forced to begin the march. Perhaps by this time, your father or brother had tried to stand up to the soldiers and had been beaten to death or run through with a sword. Perhaps your family was still clinging to each other as you were herded like abused cattle toward the Syrian Desert. Some lucky few—how lucky they were is debatable— were driven like livestock onto the cattle cars on trains. Crammed together with only standing room, they were forced to endure the long journey by rail without food or water or even somewhere to go to the bathroom. The reek of excrement must have filled those cars until the air was almost impossible to breathe. In those windowless cars, motion sickness must have been inevitable, and there was nowhere to vomit except on the people surrounding you. Sickness spread in those cars like wildfire.

Those who were not loaded onto the cars had no choice but to walk. And the distance of that walk can hardly be thought of in terms of something that any human being is capable of. The Armenians arrested in Constantinople would be forced to walk almost one thousand miles to

Deir ez-Zor. Whether they were old or young, sickly or strong, whether they had small children or grandmothers with them, or whether they were pregnant, ill, lame, or disabled, the Armenians had to move—and they had to move at a pace dictated by (comparatively) well-fed soldiers who were mostly fit young men. To fail to keep up was to be butchered brutally and with a sword. The killings by sword were done expressly to traumatize the witnesses. If you were a child, you might have to watch your parents or your siblings or your old grandparent die in a gruesome manner.

If you were a child, you were unlikely to have survived this far. The provisions that the Turkish government had made for those stumbling across the desert were utterly pitiful; in fact, the lack of provisions for food, water, or shelter that was made would later be part of the argument that what the Ottoman Empire had done was truly genocide instead of war. When the government sent those Armenians off into the desert, it was with the full knowledge that most of them would not survive. The aim was not to deport a group of rebels. The aim was to annihilate an entire cultural group.

Perhaps even worse than the starvation—which was so severe that the Armenians found themselves picking through crops for raw grains just to get something into their stomachs—was the heat. Most of the hapless victims were used to the cool, crisp air of the mountains. Now, they found themselves moving through the utter dryness of the desert without free access to potable water. They became dehydrated and died along the way in the thousands, with no shelter from the shade as they were forced to march in the heat of the day. If you were a child, clutching your mother's hand (if your mother, despite the raping and the abuse, had survived), you would see mounds of corpses lying along the roadside as you walked. Some of them would be decomposed or torn by scavenging animals. Flies would walk across their glassy eyes as they stared up at the pitiless sky, and you, a mere child, would see more death in a day than most ever see in a lifetime. Some of the corpses were buried in mass graves (60,000 Armenians were discovered in one grave alone in 1916), while others were simply left in the sun to rot.

To make matters even worse, if you were a child, you would witness the total disintegration of the mental state of many of the adults around you. Perhaps even adults that you looked up to, adults that you trusted. The psychological effects of witnessing and surviving the terror and destruction that was being wrought on their people were profound for many of the Armenians. Komitas was one of them. The mind that could pull a melody out of thin air, the heart that beat so passionately for the Armenian people, the soul that had been so wholly committed to his faith, was now reduced to a petrified shadow of itself. Komitas spent much of his time clinging to anyone he knew, babbling senselessly, every rock and boulder imagined to be a guard aiming a gun at him. He would not be the only one.

And hundreds of soldiers were either partaking in this violence and brutality or were a silent witness to it. Some of them must have felt a sense of injustice. As the bodies of innocents began to heap up by the roadside, surely there must have been some awareness that humanity had just crossed the line from warfare into something even darker. This was more than destroying a threat to national security. This was the destruction of an entire race. Yet many of them either continued to rape and kill wantonly or simply kept their mouths shut and their eyes blind to the appalling scene before them.

Armin T. Wegner, however, was not one of them. He had brought his camera to the front lines, and despite considerable threats from his superiors and the Ottomans, he used it. Smuggling the plates back home so that nobody could find them, Wegner documented the atrocities before him, despite the fact that they were being committed by his country's allies. His photographs continue the gruesome story of the death marches, images almost too heart-wrenching and too appalling to look at. A desperate and bewildered Armenian priest, overwhelmed by the number of dead for whom he wished to perform funeral rites. The skeletal corpses of children who starved to death, their bodies nothing more than bones with a thin covering of skin, their lips even drawn back from their teeth with the sparsity of their bodies. The hollow eyes of the orphans, staring blankly into the camera, the horror behind their eyes almost too much to begin to imagine. Disease sweeping through their pathetic camps and leaving behind piles of corpses.

Hundreds of thousands of Armenians died in the most horrible ways on those awful death marches. So much so that only 45,000 actually made it to Deir ez-Zor. And once they reached their destination, it would not be the end of their suffering. But Wegner was not the only voice speaking out against the destruction of the Armenian people. Thanks to the telegram, the rest of the world was listening as well.

# Chapter 8 – One Thousand Orphans

Wegner was not the only one who would raise his voice against what was happening in the Ottoman Empire. In fact, just like the missionaries who worked in the Hamidian and Adana massacres, many Americans would also speak out against the madness, sparking a wave of support in the United States as it entered WWI on the Allied side.

The American ambassador to the Ottoman Empire told his superiors how the Three Pashas had given "the death warrant to a whole race," and how even in their conversations with him, officials made no attempt to pretend that the deportation of the Armenians was anything other than a bid to exterminate them. There was no word for "genocide" in 1915, but Ambassador Henry Morgenthau's description was almost more vivid: he called it "race murder." The invention of the telegram had made it possible to transmit information across the world far more quickly than a letter, and it wasn't long before news of the genocide reached U.S. shores. The *New York Times* had already run a story about an impending massacre early in 1915, and now, it kept citizens informed of atrocity after atrocity being committed in the Ottoman Empire. Considering that the U.S. and the Ottomans were enemies during the war, it is certainly possible that some propaganda was involved. But when concerned Americans started to make an effort to help, it became clear that the story of the Armenians' fate was more than just a nightmare. It was very, very real.

The American Committee for Armenian and Syrian Relief (ACASR) was formed and was strongly supported by President Woodrow Wilson. During the genocide and especially in the years to follow, donations and volunteers flooded into the Ottoman Empire to try to help the beleaguered Armenians and other minority groups that were also being persecuted. Tragically, despite their best efforts, these volunteers were not able to do much. The Ottomans—perhaps a little surprised that some Armenians had actually made it to Deir ez-Zor—were not done yet. They would not rest until the Armenian population had been decimated.

* * * *

Ali Suad Bey could not believe his eyes.

The governor of the area around Deir ez-Zor, Ali Bey, was well versed in warfare. He was, after all, a military commander; he had seen his fair share of trouble. But nothing like this.

Ali Bey watched in utter horror as tens of thousands of Armenians came stumbling into his domain from the desert. They had just walked hundreds of miles across the Syrian Desert in midsummer, and they were all exhausted, sick, and dehydrated. Most of them were women and children; the majority of the men had been systematically killed en route. In fact, the overwhelming majority were orphaned children. They had dark, hollow eyes that seemed blank and empty thanks to the atrocities that they had witnessed, set in skeletal faces, their cheeks pinched and pale, scarred by the brutal sun. Their chapped lips were stretched thin over teeth that protruded with emaciation. All they could think about was survival. They were utterly desperate for food and water, their hair crawling with lice and wounds covering their unwashed little bodies. Ali Bey could not grasp why his government considered them such a terrible threat to national security. They were only children—traumatized, terrified, orphaned children who had endured more in the past summer than most people would ever have to see in an entire lifetime.

Ali Bey was also somewhat surprised to see them. The Turkish government had not been concerned in the slightest about what they would actually do with the Armenians once they had reached the end of the deportation; in fact, they seemed mildly surprised that any of them had survived the death marches at all. No provision whatsoever had been made to receive the deportees once they had reached Deir ez-Zor. Ali Bey was appalled and also determined to make an attempt to accommodate the 30,000 starving Armenians that were trickling onto his doorstep. There was luckily a large cave nearby that could serve as a temporary shelter from the sweltering August sun, but it could by no means accommodate that many people. Ali Bey had a real problem on his hands, and the rest of the Ottoman administration had no interest whatsoever in helping him.

Nonetheless, this courageous Arab was not about to give up on the thousands of helpless people who were now dependent on him. He strove to build refugee camps as well as he could, and for a brief time, the Armenians were provided with the rights that they had been so sorely deprived of during the death marches. Ali Bey provided them with food, water, shelter, and even medical care and protection to the best of his abilities. It could not have been easy; government funding must have been practically nonexistent for this project, and Ali Bey was almost completely alone in his efforts. To this end, he personally took in about one thousand orphans, feeding them probably out of his own pocket or possibly even plundering the coffers of the city to provide for its influx of refugees. He was determined that the Armenian Genocide—which had already claimed hundreds of thousands, if not over a million, lives on the death marches—would end with him.

If only he had been left alone to do what he was doing, Ali Bey might have succeeded, too. But it was not to be.

The Armenians, by this point, had been thrown out of the Ottoman Empire. Those who were sheltering under Ali Bey's wings were largely women and children. None of them were soldiers, and it's unlikely that any of them had shown even a smattering of rebellion. To survive the death march was to be wholly submissive; to show any spark of resistance was to die brutally in front of your watching family. Those refugees were survivors, but they were also as beaten as a human being can be. They had lost everything—their homes, businesses, jobs, families. It is inconceivable that 30,000 half-starved Armenians could be any form of a threat to the Ottoman Empire, which mobilized nearly three million soldiers during the extent of the First World War. Yet Talaat Pasha, Minister of the Interior, was not concerned with the Armenians being a threat. He hated the fact that they even existed, and this was made abundantly clear in a cipher he sent to Deir ez-Zor in September 1915. Talaat forbade the court-martial of any soldier who had committed crimes against the Armenians; he also forbade the Armenians to open any lawsuits against the Ottoman military or government.

The final straw came in mid-September 1915. By this point, the Armenians had been sheltering in Deir ez-Zor for some time, and they had established a little town of their own. Trade was starting to take place among them; they were remembering their songs and stories, their skills. They were starting to live life again despite the misery of what they had experienced—after all, the Armenians were nothing if not survivors. They were starting to find their way back to a semblance of normality, thanks to the efforts of Ali Suad Bey.

Then the orders came from Ali Bey's superior, Governor-General Abdülhalik Renda. He told Ali Bey that allowing thousands of Armenians to live peacefully in their new "home" was "an instance of disagreement with the sacred goal of the government." "Expel them from that place!" he ordered vehemently.

Ali Bey was well aware, and his superior made it clear, that their "sacred goal" was to kill every Armenian on the face of the earth. Ali Bey's response was calm and simple. "The means of transportation do not exist so that I could deport the people," he told his superior. The "means of transportation" that had been used to get them to Deir ez-Zor in the first place—the Armenians' own feet—certainly existed, but Ali Bey was making it clear that he was not going to send the refugees on another death march. He made his stance abundantly clear in the second sentence of his telegram: "If the goal being pursued is to kill them, I can neither do it, nor make it done."

Nothing was going to persuade Ali Bey to hurt the people that he was protecting. And so, he was summarily removed from his position. In his place, the Ottoman government installed Zeki Bey, a military commander who had already proven himself to be exceptionally brutal and cruel in warfare. To bully other soldiers in battle was one thing; to bully 30,000 helpless Armenians was a delight in itself in the eyes of Zeki Bey, and he fell upon his duty to make the Armenians' lives as unbearable as possible with unfettered zeal.

Under Zeki Bey, the refugee camps that Ali Bey had so lovingly set up became death camps, a harrowing precursor of what the Jewish would suffer at the hands of the Nazis in the Second World War. Food and water were immediately withheld, beatings and rapes were once again commonplace, and any fragment of hope or joy that the Armenians had found in their lives was once again removed and ruthlessly destroyed. The killings began again as thousands of children starved to death and thousands of Armenians were cast out of the camps to wander the banks of the Euphrates and die in the desert.

Saddest of all, the one thousand orphans that Ali Bey had set up in a large house and cared for personally were all thrown out onto the street. Zeki Bey did not attempt to shoot or drown them. He didn't have to. He just left them on the streets to starve. And starve they did, perhaps still begging at the doors of the home where they had so briefly found joy, until they collapsed and died in the gutters, naked and alone.

# Chapter 9 – The Black Sea Runs Red

Henry Morgenthau's image of massacred Armenian corpses. This was a common sight in the countryside of the Ottoman Empire
*https://commons.wikimedia.org/w/index.php?curid=3822803*

Eitan Belkind, Aaron Aaronsohn, and some of their associates were agronomists. At least, so the Ottoman government thought.

Eitan had been serving in the Ottoman military since he was a teenager, but he had never really been a man of war. Raised in a Jewish home, Eitan had faced discrimination similar to that suffered by his Armenian counterparts. Jews at the time feared being conscripted into the Ottoman army, but when Eitan's time came to join the military, he managed to serve in roles that didn't involve shooting a gun. First, his fluency in four different languages earned him a post as a translator. Then, in March 1915—a month before the beginning of the Armenian Genocide and after having witnessed the brutal deportation of hundreds of his own people—Eitan was assigned to work on an infestation of locusts that was sweeping across the country. Aaron Aaronsohn was the leader of this project, and Eitan became his secretary.

Now in his twenties, he was working in the city of Trebizond (modern-day Trabzon), located on the banks of the Black Sea. As a higher-ranking official, despite being a Jew, Eitan was allowed to move around the countryside more or less as he wished. He and Aaron were out in the county near the Euphrates River going about their locust-killing business in the company of some Ottoman soldiers when they saw it. A corpse. It floated quietly along, face-down, on the waters of the Euphrates. It was stripped naked, and as it floated by, Eitan could see every bone in its body. He could count the vertebrae. He could see the water lapping in the deep hollows between its ribs.

Eitan and Aaron both expressed surprise, but the Ottoman guards nearby were not flustered. They shrugged, laughing it off, saying that it was okay because it was just an Armenian. There was a camp some way up the river, and the Ottoman guards were systematically killing the Armenians—especially the orphans—by binding their hands and feet and then hurling them into the river.

The horrified Eitan would soon witness one of the most terrible mass killings that took place during the Armenian Genocide. While many of the Armenians had already died on the marches to Deir ez-Zor and other concentration camps, and many more were currently starving quietly to death, there were quicker and more popular ways of killing them, too. Driven by brainwashing and bloodlust, Turkish soldiers got more and more inventive with their methods of murdering the Armenians by the hundreds. Merely shooting them seemed far too merciful for so dangerous and evil a people as the Armenians; instead, they took to dousing them (especially orphans) in gasoline and then setting them on fire. Drowning was also popular, and here in Trebizond, the killers were spoiled as they could choose between the Euphrates and the Black Sea.

Eitan made it his mission to find out what was happening to the Armenians, and what he saw was horrifying. His eyewitness account describes the most terrible scenes: the appalling concentration camps, where his Armenian friend, Shirinyan, found his own family starving to death; the screams of women, heard in the night, and the later discovery of beheaded children floating in the bloodstained Euphrates; Arab sheiks pawing through Armenian women to find wives (whose husbands would be slaughtered once the sheik made his choice, if they hadn't been killed already) as their people were being murdered within sight of them; the burning of five thousand Armenians tied to a pile of blazing dry grass.

But worst of all was a scene witnessed from the banks of the Black Sea itself. A scene that would see the Black Sea's waters turn crimson.

* * * *

In Eitan's wanderings among the Armenians, their awful plight must have sparked in him a dark suspicion: someone, some specific person in the government of Trebizond and its surroundings, must be behind all of this. That man was Cemal Azmi, the governor of Trebizond.

Before the genocide began in earnest, Azmi had been one of the founders of the so-called Special Organization. Officially, the Special Organization existed chiefly to reopen Parliament after it was closed by Abdul Hamid, but it continued after the reopening with one cold goal: to suppress the enemies of the Ottoman Empire. And now that the empire had deemed the Armenians its enemies, many members of the Special Organization were now among the chief perpetrators of the genocide.

Azmi was no exception. He earned his nickname "the butcher of Trebizond" by ordering many of the awful killings that Eitan had witnessed, including the burning of those five thousand people outside Trebizond. But the gruesome burnings, drownings, and shootings of innocent and unarmed people were not Azmi's only methods of disposing of the Armenians that he hated so much. He had more insidious ways—ways to get to those lucky handfuls of Armenians that had not been deported at all, ways to strike at them right where they felt safest: in the hospital for routine vaccinations or procedures.

At the time, typhus was sweeping through the war-torn empire, particularly in the concentration camps or areas impoverished by decades of massacre and war. In the modern day, typhus is treatable with antibiotics. In the winter of 1914 to 1916, decades before the discovery of penicillin, it was a death sentence even to fairly healthy people; to the starved and stressed victims of genocide, it was almost invariably fatal.

To many, the typhus epidemic was just a tragedy upon all the other tragedies that were taking place in the empire, but to Azmi, it was potentially a weapon. Normally spread by human body lice (which were utterly abundant in the concentration camps), typhus could also be spread purposefully by other means, and Azmi quickly persuaded some of the doctors at the Trebizond Red Crescent Hospital to carry out the dirty deed. Under the pretense of giving routine vaccinations, a handful of doctors at the hospital started drawing blood from patients who were sick and feverish with typhoid. Then, when Armenians who were due to be deported came into the hospital, they were given that disease-ridden blood. Artificially assisted in this way, the typhus epidemic became even more rampant. And the bacteria causing the disease was not the only thing that the doctors were giving the innocent people—particularly children—who came into the hospital. Countless children were overdosed with morphine to the point that they died. The doctors, who had been educated in order to help people, were killing them by the hundreds.

But it wasn't good enough for Azmi. Perhaps the doctors simply weren't killing enough people; perhaps the reason for Azmi's impatience was darker than that. Given his penchant for killing children, perhaps Azmi was driven by bloodlust to the extent that he wanted to see the Armenians suffer. Irritated by the hospital's methodical eradication of its Armenian patients, Azmi ordered thousands of Armenian women and children (there were very few men left alive by this point) to be rounded up and taken to the docks.

Once these innocent people had been taken to the shores, they were told that they were being deported to another town across the Black Sea. Figuring that being deported from one hellish area to another couldn't be any worse than staying in Trebizond, the people climbed on board the ships and waited as they were taken out upon the icy winter waters of the Black Sea. But they would never see the other side. When they were some distance out to sea, the ships were stopped, and their crews started seizing the women and children. Their screams echoed out across the frigid water, chilling the bones of all those who watched in dread from the shore, as they were cast into the sea. Their shrieks turned to gasps then to splutters and coughs as the icy sea began to overwhelm them. Some of the stronger ones tried to swim and clawed at the flanks of the great ships screaming for help or mercy, ripping out their fingernails trying to make their way back on the ships. But the crews just laughed, grabbed the children, and threw them overboard. Some of the desperate women must have tried to save those children; others, drowning, panicking, must have seized their fellow Armenians and dragged them under in their dying terror. The cold water was quick to paralyze many of them. Their shrieks reached a climax when the crews had thrown most of them into the water and started sailing back, leaving them thrashing and floundering with no hope of making it to the shore. But as they drowned in the thousands, the eerie screaming that echoed across the Black Sea's waves diminished. Eventually, the last set of waving arms above the water became still, and the last desperate, thrashing woman was overwhelmed by the waves. Silence fell, and the silence was infinitely worse than the screaming.

* * * *

While many of those who witnessed the atrocities in Trebizond simply remained silent, complicit in the genocide by their unwillingness to speak against it—or perhaps terrified into silence by the fear that something similar would happen to them—these events are known to history because of a courageous handful of Ottoman citizens who were brave enough to testify against those who perpetrated these unspeakable crimes. Among them were doctors at the hospital who had to watch in disgust as their colleagues killed innocent children, foreign ambassadors, and even members of the government who were unable to stop the killing but would later appear in court to tell of the terrible things that had happened. Most of these would testify years after the end of the First World War. But one small group of people was feeding information constantly to the British, telling them about the Ottomans' plans, about the killing of the Armenians and other minority groups. And Eitan Belkind was among them.

The truth was that while almost everyone thought he was simply a harmless agronomist seeking to save Ottoman crops from the ravaging locusts, nothing could be further from the truth. Eitan had always had a fire inside him, a desire to see justice done for his fellow Jews and other minorities. And that fire caused him to co-found, alongside his friend Aaron Aaronsohn, a secret organization known as NILI.

NILI was an acronym for "Netzah Yisrael Lo Yeshaker," Hebrew for "The Eternal One of Israel will not lie," and it was a Jewish spy ring that worked for the British in a bid to bring down the Ottoman Empire. Israel, the homeland of the Jewish people, had been under Ottoman occupation for four hundred years; now, the much-oppressed Jews were being deported from their ancient homeland just like the Armenians, and Aaron and Eitan were determined to make it stop. The simplest way to do so would be to get the British who were based in Egypt to invade the Ottoman Empire and liberate Israel. For years, Aaron, Eitan, and their fellow NILI spies had been traveling across the empire under the pretense of being government agronomists, gathering information to help the Ottomans' enemies.

It was a homing pigeon that eventually brought down NILI in late 1917, more than a year after the mass drownings at Trebizond. It landed on the wrong rooftop, and the Turkish governor who lived in the home was able to crack the code in the encrypted message it carried. The NILI members were rounded up, jailed, and sentenced to death. But while they languished in jail, in December 1917, the British used the information that NILI had provided to invade Palestine and take back Jerusalem, liberating it from four centuries of Ottoman rule. As for Eitan, he and some of his fellow NILI members were able to escape from jail as the Turks fled from the advancing British. Eitan's testimony about the Armenians became a key part of allowing the world to know what had really happened and of finding justice for the perpetrators. With his work done, Eitan was able to live out his life as a peaceful agronomist (for real this time), and he died in 1979 having lived a long and full life.

But by the time the British took Palestine, it was, of course, far too late for the Armenians. Back at the start of 1916, they were still being butchered by the hundreds. And it would be a long time before their suffering would finally be at an end.

# Chapter 10 – Stolen Children

The more Armenian men and women that they killed, the larger a single problem grew for the Ottoman Empire: what to do with the orphans that remained.

Azmi, of course, had his own way of dealing with the children—namely, injecting them with deadly bacteria or giving them an opioid overdose, burning them, and throwing them into the Black Sea. However, none of those ways were really profitable. All the good Armenian plunder had already been taken by the time the terrified and helpless orphans were killed in the thousands. Azmi wanted more than just death; he wanted money and pleasure too, and like other perpetrators of the genocide, he would find both in the waves of orphans that came into Trebizond.

Perhaps one of the greatest atrocities that Azmi committed was to use the orphans as sex slaves—often ten or more at a time—and then have them killed afterward. His son likely did the same when Azmi picked out thirteen of the prettiest young Armenian girls and gave them to the young man as a gift. Tragically, this was not unusual, and orphans were not the only targets. Armenian women and children were stolen from their own families and sold off as sex slaves; girls were raped and then forced to join the harems of important and brutal Turkish men.

Not all of those abducted would be forced into sex slavery, however. Some would have a different core element of themselves taken away from them: the faith that they and their families had practiced for generations.

Sold or abducted into Muslim families, the Armenian women and children would be stripped of everything that their race had stood for since ancient times. They were forbidden to speak their own language or to worship according to their own beliefs; instead, they were held down as Islamic tattoos were forced onto their bodies. To many of them, who had been raised in a completely different religion, the experience must have been akin to rape—the rape of one's very soul. Forced into silence and threatened with death, they were made to practice a faith they did not believe in. Even worse, they must have been treated harshly, even though they had been forcibly "converted." They were little more than slaves in these Muslim households, and Armenian women who had been married off to Turkish men were forbidden to own any property.

Not all of the Armenian-Turkish marriages were things of grief and hatred, however. In fact, many Turks were determined to save as many Armenian women as they could by marrying them, which would make them off-limits to the marauding Ottoman soldiers. Eitan Belkind wrote of one Turkish man who had married five Armenian wives to save them from the genocide.

Some Armenian families were so desperate, faced with deportation and/or brutal execution, that they voluntarily gave up their children to their Muslim friends or neighbors—assuming they had any left that didn't want to kill them. Even though they knew their children would be raised as followers of Islam, at least they wouldn't be exiled and/or killed. Whether they had been abducted or voluntarily given up, many of these children were nonetheless mistreated, used simply for their labor and with many of the girls put into harems. They were forced to abandon their faith and the language they'd been born into, and the national identity that the Armenians had been clinging to for so many years was quietly wiped away. Their very culture was in danger of annihilation.

After the genocide, rescue missions would reveal the atrocities that these enslaved women and children had to endure at the hands of their brutal masters. Some men had vast numbers of sex slaves at their command; one record states of a Muslim man who "owned" twelve underage Armenian girls. Their rescuers could only get them back by buying them, as if they were sheep or cattle.

Children, women, and lives were not the only things that the Turks were taking from their Armenian neighbors, however. Armenians had wealth and property too—and many greedy Turks were determined to get their hands on it.

* * * *

Ahmed Riza could not believe his ears.

A fiercely handsome man in his sixties, Ahmed Riza was a man of many talents. A scientist, mathematician, and proficient politician, he had joined the Young Turk Revolution and become one of the most prominent members of the CUP. At the time of the First World War, the President of the Senate was only one of his many titles, and he was intimately involved in the workings of Parliament.

Ahmed Riza had seen a lot of trouble in his time. He had been a witness to the Armenian massacres in the preceding years, and even now, he was well aware of the deportations that were occurring throughout the empire. Unlike most representatives of Parliament, however, Ahmed Riza was not comfortable with the deportation of the

Armenians. And now he could not believe what the CUP's Central Committee was saying.

When the Armenians were first deported, they had been given ten days to carry out an ultimatum imposed upon them by the Ottoman government—an ultimatum that may have even brought a flicker of hope to the victims of the deportations. They were told to close up their homes and businesses exactly as they were, taking nothing and certainly selling nothing; their money was all to be deposited into the bank under the name of friends or relatives from abroad, and they were to leave behind all of their possessions. Livestock and buildings, fields and crops, equipment and machinery, furniture and appliances, cups and plates and forks, beds and pillows and pets—they were all to be left just as they were. The Ottoman government assured the Armenians that this would be so that everything could be preserved exactly as it was for their eventual return to their homes once the war was over. Perhaps the Armenians felt a stirring of hope and comfort at the thought of leaving everything as it was. Perhaps they believed that they would be returning to the lives they had built for themselves in the empire that didn't want them.

Or perhaps they were already suspicious. Perhaps they already knew what was coming.

By September 1915, vast numbers of Armenians had been murdered or exiled, and the towns and villages were filled with shops and houses whose empty windows stared out onto the street like the dead eyes of their former owners left in the desert. The sheer amount of property and capital that had been left behind was simply overwhelming, and the Ottoman government, now knowing that those Armenians were never coming back, was able to implement a scheme that may have been in play since the beginning, a scheme to give the Armenians' considerable wealth to new, Muslim owners. This may have been part of the motivation for the Armenian Genocide from the very beginning, and now it came to its dreadful fruition as the CUP passed the Temporary Law of Expropriation and Confiscation. This law was better known by its sickly euphemism, the "Abandoned Properties" law. Its decree was simple and awful: all properties owned by dead or deported Armenians would immediately be confiscated and become the property of the Ottoman government.

Ahmed Riza was utterly appalled. He knew that naming it the Abandoned Properties Law was simply inaccurate. These properties had not been abandoned, he argued; they had been left behind when their owners were forcibly cast out of their homes and businesses and forced to walk hundreds of miles across the desert to their deaths. Despite the controversy that would undoubtedly surround his support of the hated Armenians, Ahmed Riza was loud in his opposition of the law.

"[The Armenians] were forcibly, compulsorily removed from their domiciles and exiled!" he protested. "Now the government through its efforts is selling their goods...This is atrocious! Grab my arm, eject me from my village, then sell my goods and properties? Such a thing can never be permissible. Neither the conscience of the Ottomans nor the law can allow it."

Ahmed Riza's loud argument was well substantiated too. He drew on articles of the constitution to prove why it was unlawful for the Abandoned Properties Law to be passed, but it was all to no avail. The single parliamentary champion of the victims of the genocide had vastly overestimated both the Ottoman conscience and the willingness of the CUP to adhere to the law. The Abandoned Properties Law was passed, and all Armenian assets were immediately seized by the government.

Some of these Armenian properties were sold off to Muslim Turks, often at a tiny fraction of their worth. Others were expropriated for warfare and poured into the slowly failing effort of the Central Powers to stand against the Allies. Either way, they would never be returned to the Armenians who were still alive. The Turks made their best effort to erase every trace of the Armenian culture from their towns and villages, making it feel as though the people had not only been destroyed but also forgotten.

Just as the savage guards had stripped the Armenian corpses of their clothes and left the dead men, women, and children naked in the dunes and gutters during the death march, the Armenian government had now torn away everything that the Armenians owned. And to this day, that property has not been returned to the families of its rightful owners. The vice president of Turkey lives in a mansion that once belonged to a wealthy Armenian, Ohannes Kasabian. Kasabian had the money to flee from the genocide and survive its wrath, but upon his return, he found that the stately home where he had once lived in tranquil prosperity had been confiscated. He would never live in his own house again. And until 2018, the leaders of Turkey had made it their official residence. Their equivalent of the White House was built on stolen ground. And after the genocide, the Turkish nation was rebuilt after the First World War on the lands of the Armenians that it had annihilated.

* * * *

To this day, reparations for the genocide have largely not been made to the descendants of the Armenians that survived it. The property confiscated by the Turkish government—the value of which today would be more than three hundred billion U.S. dollars—has remained in the clutches of those who took it, and the Armenians had to start over from scratch, even though they once made up a large proportion of the Ottoman middle class. In some ways, justice has still not been served.

But after years of relentless killings, the Armenians would start to see the light at the end of the tunnel. The destruction of their people was part of the death throes of an empire that was about to be destroyed itself. Relief was coming, but for millions of Armenians, that relief would be too late.

# Chapter 11 – Justice

Fall had come gently to the Greek island of Lemnos. Admiral Arthur Gough-Calthorpe, standing on the deck of the British warship *Agamemnon*, couldn't help but admire the deep blue tinge of the water in the port of Mudros. The balmy October sun was still much warmer than he was used to back in England, but he knew that in summer the sun burned with a savagery that the pale-skinned British were wholly unprepared for.

The day was October 30th, 1918, and Calthorpe couldn't help but think back to this time three years earlier when hundreds of thousands of British soldiers were about to enter a bitter winter on the rocky peninsula of Gallipoli, Greece. They had used Lemnos as a staging ground for the invasion of Gallipoli, full of hope that taking the Dardanelles Strait would allow the British, French, and Australian troops to meet up with their Russian allies in the Black Sea, cutting Turkey in half and allowing the Allies to destroy the Ottoman resistance. Yet Gallipoli had proven to be one of the harshest front lines of the entire war—and one of the most humiliating defeats suffered by the

British during the First World War.

Winston Churchill had been just a Lord Admiral then, and Gallipoli became known as one of his greatest blunders. Calthorpe could not have known that Churchill would someday become the prime minister who led Britain through a war even greater than the one in which Calthorpe was fighting right now; back in 1918, a war bigger than the so-called Great War was practically incomprehensible. Yet Calthorpe could feel the sense of relief that was starting to spread across the world for the first time in four years of utterly brutal warfare. The war was ending, and the Allies were coming out on top.

That was why Calthorpe had chosen to anchor the *Agamemnon* in the waters of Lemnos. It was a kind of symbolism to show the Turks how far the British had come since the disaster that had been Gallipoli in 1915. Plagued by heat, flies, dysentery, difficult terrain, and the appallingly unhygienic conditions, almost a quarter of a million Allied soldiers had become casualties of the Gallipoli front. They had taken the same number of Turks with them, but nonetheless, the British had had no choice but to evacuate in January of 1916. Yet that had not been the end of the British invasion of the Ottoman Empire's domains. Forcing their way through the Middle East—aided by Eitan Belkind and other members of NILI—the British had claimed many of the empire's Arab territories. By October 30th, 1918, the once-mighty Ottoman Empire had been brought to its knees. One cannot help but speculate on how things may have been different for the empire if it had concentrated more of its money and manpower on fighting the war with its enemies rather than butchering its innocents.

Now, Admiral Arthur Calthorpe was only a few minutes away from signing the Mudros Armistice with Turkish Minister of the Navy Rauf Orbay. He had taken Djemal Pasha's place as minister when Djemal had fled to Germany, knowing that he had committed more crimes than simply fighting his enemies in the war. He was guilty of much more than that.

He was guilty of genocide. And he would be condemned for it.

* * * *

Less than two weeks after the signing of the Mudros Armistice, which acknowledged the Ottoman defeat and their surrender to the British Empire, Germany also signed an armistice with the Allies on November 11ᵗʰ, 1918. A ceasefire was called, and the ugly mess that had been the First World War at last ground to a halt.

The aftermath was almost unthinkable, not least within the Ottoman Empire. As the Allies started to move through the empire, they were appalled that the reports of what was being done to the Armenians had all been true. The Mudros Armistice had forced the Ottomans to hand over all the surviving Armenian prisoners to the Allies; the stories they told were horrific, and the fact that there were so few of them was more horrific still. Before the First World War, two million Armenians had made their homes in the Ottoman Empire. By the end of it, when the genocide finally ceased, there were only about 400,000 left. Around one and a half million Armenians had died.

Clearly, something would have to be done. The people who had committed these atrocious crimes would be brought to justice, and so, a series of trials began in order to find and punish the perpetrators of the genocide.

The Allies had ordered Sultan Mehmed VI, who was (to his surprise) still on the throne, to organize courts-martial for the leading members of the CUP. They would be tried for entering the First World War on the side of the Central Powers but also for crimes against humanity committed in the form of the Armenian Genocide. Of course, the three people that the Allies were really after were not in the Ottoman Empire at the time. The Three Pashas had fled to Germany before the war ended, abandoning the empire they had so thoroughly desecrated.

While some of the trials were held in Trebizond—the city that had witnessed the gruesome mass drownings in the Black Sea—others were held in Constantinople. The fact that the Three Pashas were not present to be tried was not enough to stop the Allies from trying. They were tried in absentia at Constantinople in July 1919.

At the time, after years of turmoil and warfare, the Ottomans were a crushed and broken-spirited people. The rest of the world was appalled at the atrocities that the Ottomans had committed, and finally, the greater Turkish population of the empire was confronted with the blood that was on their hands. And while it was mainly soldiers who had done the killing, a truly tragic number of civilians had taken part too. They had formed gangs to oust the Armenians from their homes, and the more criminal elements had taken to killing, raping, and looting. Turks had adopted children whose parents had been slaughtered; they had bought the sex slaves that were a lucrative byproduct of the genocide. And even those who had not been directly involved in the genocide were living in Armenian houses and running businesses taken from the hands of dead men and women. And now that it was all over, the Turks became suddenly and terribly aware of what their people had done.

A pang of collective guilt flooded across the nation, filling the hearts and minds of the Turkish people. While the aftermath of the genocide could not be exactly termed as mourning, it was undoubtedly true that the Turks became aware of how terrible the treatment of the Armenians truly had been. Some of this guilt even made its way into the government. Spurred on by the Allied administration that was keeping a close eye on the proceedings, the court dealt ruthlessly with the cases of the Three Pashas. All three of them were condemned to death, the CUP was dissolved, and the properties of its members were confiscated by the state. In fact, these trials were the first time that the concept of a crime against humanity was introduced.

Sadly, however, as 1919 turned into 1920, it became evident that the early zeal of the Turkish court was starting to lose its fervor. Sultan Mehmed VI was too nervous to prosecute the powerful Young Turks; they had exerted a reign of terror over him as well as over the people, and where a strong sultan might have led the Ottoman Empire forth into the light of day, their ruler failed them by cowering in terror, fearing a revolution. More than 130 high-ranking government officials had been arrested for the trials, and yet the sentencing was not taking place the way it was supposed to. The British intervened when little had been done by May 1920 and moved the proceedings to the more neutral ground of Malta, where it was expected that the Allies would deliver swift justice to the guilty. But it was not to be. The Turkish courts, possibly on purpose, had so befuddled the case and bungled the necessary documents that the trials could not proceed. Only a handful of the vast numbers of guilty administrators were ever sentenced, and no reparations would ever be made to the Armenian people from whom everything had been taken, even though originally the Allies had attempted to force the Ottoman Empire to give Armenia its independence.

The revolution that had so crippled Mehmed's resolve took place after all. In 1921, as the Malta tribunals were wading forth through a quagmire of red tape and messy laws, Mustafa Kemal Atatürk turned his slow-growing nationalist revolution into a direct threat to the British. He took a group of British people hostage, demanding that the political prisoners being held for the tribunals should be freed. Winston Churchill, at that time the secretary of war, had bigger problems on his hands than the mess of the Ottoman Empire. He let the prisoners go and left the Ottoman Empire at the mercy of Atatürk. Atatürk had none. Finding support in Soviet Russia, he launched a violent military struggle against the leadership of the empire, seeking his own power. Those Armenians that remained—some of whom had not been deported during the genocide—armed themselves and attempted to stand against him. They were crushed and massacred in what became known as the Turkish-Armenian War of 1920, adding thousands more to the death toll.

When the British withdrew from the Ottoman Empire, Atatürk picked up right where the Three Pashas left off. Atatürk was elected president of the new Republic of Turkey—the Ottoman Empire, by this time, had been dissolved—and he started deporting more and more Armenians again. However, this time, there was no real religious motivation behind their deportations. Atatürk transformed Turkey into a secular country, closing the Islamic schools and organizations and forming the new republic into something far more modern than the carcass of the Ottoman Empire from which it risen.

As for the Armenians, they would continue to suffer until 1923. By then, there were hardly any of them left to kill, and the genocide tapered off as the Republic of Turkey started to find its feet.

In the wake of the genocide, the Armenians started to find their feet once again, trying to put together their lives even after everything they once had was taken away from them. And the thing they wanted back the most may just have been their children. The children who had been kidnapped and assimilated into Muslim households were still out there, some of them having almost forgotten their Armenian identity (it had, after all, been eight years since the killing started). But others were being held against their will, wanting to get back to their homes and families.

Only a few hundred thousand Armenians remained in Turkey; most of them had fled to other countries and formed diaspora communities there, where, despite the suffering they had endured because of it, they continued to practice their ways and live in their culture. Their national identity had not been crushed by the genocide.

It had only been strengthened.

# Chapter 12 – Operation Nemesis

Armin T. Wegner in 1916
*https://commons.wikimedia.org/w/index.php?curid=30310497*

It had been a long time since the Armenians had really had a hero. Ali Bey, protecting thousands of refugees in Syria, had come close; so had Eitan Belkind, who fed information to the Allies, and Armin T. Wegner, who helped to document the atrocities. But the next heroes who would rise up in the aftermath of the unthinkable genocide were not Arabic, Jewish, German. They were Armenian themselves, and they were seeking justice after witnessing the heartless desecration of their people.

One of them was Ruben Heryan. Having emigrated to the United States as a young man, Ruben could have done what thousands of Armenian Americans—and other foreigners —did about the genocide: sit back and shake their head grimly at the grisly articles in the *New York Times* or maybe donate a little extra money to the "poor starving children in Armenia." Ruben was well-off, well-respected, and well-liked in the community; there was no way that the genocide of his people could have caused him direct danger where he lived in New York. But he could not watch them die. By 1918, while the war was still raging, he had gathered a group of volunteers to join the Armenian Legion, a legion within the French Army, and made his way into the heart of the Ottoman Empire. His mission was simple: rescue.

It proved not to be as simple as Ruben had hoped. 1918 was a frustrating year for him. He was in his fifties already, and although his cheerful demeanor and can-do attitude had earned him the nickname of "the young man with the gray hair," he was no longer capable of fighting on the front lines. While his younger fellow volunteers were sent to the front lines, Ruben was stuck in Cairo, guarding a hospital. Perhaps it was in the hospital that he found his true passion, serving and saving the helpless. His heart was turned toward those Armenians who had been kidnapped into families they didn't know and forced to be someone that they weren't. He thought of the women and children who had been abducted or sold into Muslim homes, and he was determined to get them back.

Once the Three Pashas had fled the empire, Ruben was able to launch his rescue mission in earnest. Traveling the length and breadth of the empire from Deir ez-Zor to Constantinople, he started to raise funds in order to save the kidnapped Armenians. His heartfelt account of the generosity of his own people evokes both pity and respect; while the wealthy Armenians who had escaped the genocide were able to give sizable donations, some of the money that Ruben managed to raise came from utterly penniless victims of the genocide. They were still leaving the concentration camps, riddled with lice, sick, skeletal, and with only a couple of coins to their name. But when they heard of the women and children being held by the Muslims, they felt that these strangers' plights were worst and so gave their last scraps of money to Ruben and his team.

Every penny they could collect was desperately needed. The Muslims would not give up their Armenian captives easily; they hid their identities or smuggled them out to secret locations, making the searches almost impossible in many instances. Ruben spent months, sometimes years, seeking for specific women or children. Once they were found, almost the only way to get them back was to buy them. The whole operation was costly in terms of finances, but it was even more costly in emotional terms. Ruben brokenly described how some of the captives he discovered had seemed to have forgotten who they really were. Fully grown women, who could no longer speak Armenian, had wiped away the traces of their ethnicity in a bid to survive. Children who could not remember their real parents clung to their Muslim adopters. There were sex slaves who were too frightened to speak up for themselves or open up to their rescuers. Stockholm syndrome would inevitably have been a tragic part of Ruben's mission.

The genocide would end in a few years, but in many ways, it lived on forever in the minds of those it had so brutally afflicted. Komitas was one of them. Even though he had returned to Constantinople and did not have to suffer the horrors of the concentration camps at Deir ez-Zor, he would never recover from the post-traumatic stress disorder that the deportation and death marches had given him. He was shuttled from one psychiatric hospital to the other for the rest of his life until he died in 1935.

* * * *

Ruben Heryan was one of the very first heroes of the Armenian Genocide. He worked tirelessly to find, save, and protect captive Armenians in what became known as the Liberation Mission, giving them the chance to grow up the way they had been born: Armenian. He freed them from the often cruel and oppressive clutches of those who had bought or abducted them, and he gave them a chance to live a new and different life on their own terms.

Other Armenian heroes, however, would not be as gentle or devoted as Ruben was. Their mission would not be rescue. It would be justice, and if the rest of the world was not going to carry out the Three Pashas' death sentences, then one group of Armenians decided that it would have to be their duty.

The Armenian Revolutionary Federation, which had pledged its alliance to the CUP when it was first formed, had been thoroughly kicked in the teeth for its attempt to mend fences with the Turkish back in 1908 before the Young Turk Revolution. Many of its members had been among those intellectuals arrested on April 24th, 1915, the eve of the genocide. Others had escaped and survived, however, and the ARF had been responsible for the resistance that had sparked the Turkish-Armenian War in 1920.

Now that the wars were over, the ARF turned its focus to gaining justice after the genocide. It was decided that there was only one way to do this: to find and kill those who had perpetrated the genocide. A blacklist was made, 200 names long, of those who had been the guiltiest. Some of the most important of these were the Three Pashas and Cemal Azmi, the Butcher of Trebizond.

Shahan Natalie was the leader of the group, which dubbed themselves Operation Nemesis. From their headquarters in Watertown, Massachusetts, Nemesis started to put together a plan to eliminate the enemies of the Armenian people. And the most important of them all was Talaat Pasha. Talaat had been so deeply bent on destroying every living Armenian, innocent or not, that he had ordered Ali Suad Bey to kill 30,000 starving and terrified refugees. Talaat had wanted the entire nation dead, and now that nation demanded his death, too.

On March 15th, 1921, the death sentence that had been laid upon Talaat in 1918 was finally carried out but not by an executioner. Instead, it was done by a young, handsome, dark-eyed engineering student named Soghomon Tehlirian.

Like practically every surviving Armenian, Soghomon was haunted by the memories of his family and how they had died in the thoughtless brutality of the genocide. His mother, in particular, had been beheaded in the genocide. To make matters worse, Soghomon had epilepsy, and the fear of a seizure coming upon him at any moment had made life difficult from the start. Still, he wanted to move on with his life. He wanted to settle down and marry his girlfriend Anihad, whom he loved more than anything. Yet the memory of his family, the knowledge that they would never have the peaceful life that he could lead in the United States, was intolerable. He had to do something. He had to *kill* something; he had to take from someone what had been taken from him. So, when Shahan Natalie looked into his dark, turbulent eyes, he knew he was looking at someone whose love and agony could make them a deadly force to be reckoned with.

In 1921, Operation Nemesis flew Soghomon out to Berlin, where Talaat Pasha had been hiding for the three years since he had fled the Ottoman Empire. For months, deeply undercover and sharing a room with some students, Soghomon studied his neighbor across the street, Talaat Pasha, the man who had murdered three-quarters of the Armenian race. To all appearances, Talaat was no one of importance. He had grown out his beard, and he lived a quiet life between his two burly bodyguards, and he liked nothing more than taking a soothing morning stroll at precisely 11:00 a.m. in the park.

The stroll was his fatal mistake. Arming himself with a Luger pistol on a nippy spring morning, Soghomon quietly began to follow Talaat from his residence. It was all he could do to stay calm as he walked in the very footsteps of the man who had ordered the deaths of hundreds of thousands, of the man who had killed his mother. Soghomon had not been in Armenia during the genocide (despite what he would later say at his trial), but he did have one particularly vivid and painful memory from that period: he had joined the Russian army in the liberation of Van from its siege in 1915, and while with the army, he had come across a little girl running through the woods, crying relentlessly. When Soghomon grabbed her, he was shocked to recognize her pale, dirty face. It was his niece, Armenouhi. She had just witnessed the genocide.

It was the memory of his mother's smile, of Armenouhi's terrified cries, that spurred Soghomon to do what he did next. He took the pistol out of his coat and cried out one word. "Talaat!"

Talaat Pasha turned, a flash of fear crossing his face. Soghomon raised the pistol and gave Talaat what he had denied thousands of Armenians that were drowned or burned during the genocide: an instantaneous death. Blood sprayed from Talaat's neck, and he fell to the ground.

The crowd around Soghomon immediately started shrieking, the bodyguards rushing toward him. When Natalie had given Soghomon his orders, his words had been blunt: "You blow up the skull of the Number One nation-murderer and you don't try to flee," he had said. "You stand there, your foot on the corpse and surrender to the police."

Soghomon knew that a public trial was part of Operation Nemesis' plan to draw awareness to the genocide. In the face of the charging crowd, however, he tried to flee. He didn't get far. The mob pulled him down and started to pummel him, and Soghomon might not have made it out alive if the German police hadn't been able to rescue him. The German police arrested him and took him to jail, and so began one of the most sensational trials the world had yet seen at that point.

By 1921, even though the Armenian Genocide would not officially be over until about 1923, the world had moved on from worrying about the Armenians and had started worrying about the aftermath of the world war in general. The brutal trench warfare had had a devastating effect on the global psyche, and the whole world had been changed by the conflict. The Armenians had started to become yesterday's problem, and Operation Nemesis was determined to change that. Soghomon's trial was an integral part of that plan.

As Soghomon had committed the crime in Berlin, it was considered a German matter, and so, he was tried in a German court. This turned out to work in Soghomon's favor. Germany was starting to feel the guilt of being associated with the Ottoman Empire and not doing anything to stop the genocide, and Soghomon's testimony of what had been done to the Armenians not only captured the attention of the world, but it also touched the jurors' hearts profoundly. True to Operation Nemesis' goal of sensationalizing the genocide, Soghomon's testimony was wildly embellished, especially considering that he had not actually been a witness to the deaths of his family, but it could have easily been the tale of any young Armenian who had suffered at the hands of the Turks.

Soghomon also related how he had suffered numerous nervous breakdowns after the massacres, something that may well have been true and something that his defense attorney was quick to note. The most striking moment of the trial came when the judge turned to Soghomon—who was on the stand—just after the indictment was read and asked him for his answer to the indictment. Soghomon answered that his answer was negative.

"But, prior to this trial, you thought differently," said the judge. "You admitted that you had premeditated the act."

His defense attorney requested that the judge direct his next question to Soghomon. "Why do you consider yourself not guilty?" "Because my conscience is clear," he stated.

"Why is your conscience clear?" asked the judge.

"Because I have killed a man." Soghomon squared his shoulders. "But I am not a murderer."

After only a two day trial, the jury voted in agreement of Soghomon's statement. Armin T. Wegner was one of the witnesses testifying about the atrocities of the genocide, and his testimony was a key part of Soghomon's eventual acquittal. Despite abundant eyewitnesses and evidence that Soghomon had decided to shoot Talaat Pasha and done so with premeditated intent, he was acquitted of all crimes and allowed to go free; even his pistol was given back to him. Officially, he had been acquitted because of a plea of temporary insanity. But the whole world got the sense that the jury agreed with Soghomon that justice had been served. In the words of a *New York Times* headline, "They had to let him go."

# Chapter 13 – Denial

Talaat Pasha was not the only victim of Operation Nemesis. The operation pledged to cleanse the world of the stain of those who had perpetrated the genocide, just as those perpetrators had "cleansed" the empire of one and a half million souls, and the group made good on its promise.

Berlin was the scene of another pair of grisly assassinations. One of the victims was the leader of the Special Organization and a founder of the CUP, Behaeddin Shakir; the other was Djemal Azmi, the man who had butchered thousands at Trebizond. In Tbilisi, Cemal Pasha—the second of the Three Pashas, the one who had overseen the death marches—was killed as well. With two of the Three Pashas dead, Operation Nemesis only had one left to deal with: Enver Pasha, the fanatically warlike ex-Minister of War. But it turned out that when it came to assassinating Enver, Nemesis had to get in line. Fellow Armenians, employed by the Soviet Cheka (secret police), beat them to it. And so, despite the fact that none of them would ever face an official executioner, all three of the Pashas eventually got the death sentence that was coming to them.

In total, during the two years of its existence, Operation Nemesis was responsible for the killing of seven condemned perpetrators of the genocide and three Armenian traitors who had led the Turks to the doorsteps of their own people. Turkey, then and now, portrayed Nemesis as a terrorist organization; considering the grief that Nemesis wrought on the families of the men it killed and that it denied the men their chance at redemption in the eyes of the world, Nemesis can hardly be considered as a heroic operation. Yet there was a sense of international relief that the Three Pashas were finally dead.

Nemesis was as short-lived as it was controversial. In 1922, facing pressure after Armenia fell under the control of the Soviet Union, Operation Nemesis was disbanded. It had achieved its primary goal, and its chilling reign over the lives of the men with blood on their hands had left many more men with blood on theirs. Mercifully, the circle of revenge and killing more or less ended there.

Soghomon, according to those who knew him, did not find true peace in killing Talaat. However, his relentless wanderings came to an end, and he was able to settle down and marry the girl that he loved so much. They settled in Yugoslavia, where, many years later, Soghomon eventually threw the gun that had killed Talaat Pasha into the Danube River. He died an old man with grandchildren, something that his decisions had denied Talaat.

\* \* \* \*

When it comes to the Armenian Genocide, denial seems to be the overarching theme.

Despite the world's initial horror at what was taking place in Armenia, the governments of various countries were slow to officially recognize what had truly happened, perhaps in light of Atatürk's rising power. In fact, there wasn't even a word for what the CUP had done to the

Armenian race. "Massacre" or "nation-murder" were the terms that were used at the time, but "massacre" hardly seemed big enough to encompass the extermination of an entire race, and "nation-murder" felt clumsy. And so, the world stumbled around the terrible weight of the bloodstained elephant in the room that the genocide had become.

Meanwhile, the "war to end all wars" had not brought about the peace that the world so desperately needed. Instead, tensions only escalated. In 1939, just 21 years after the end of the First World War, conflict erupted across the entire world again. Soldiers from all over the world would be dragged into the various theaters of the Second World War, from Japan to South Africa, from the United States to Germany, from Australia to the ever-growing Soviet Union. And like the First World War, this would see a number of despotic rulers rise to power. Most infamous among them was Adolf Hitler.

Hitler was determined to do to Germany, which had been flailing under the punitive measures imposed by the Allies ever since the Treaty of Versailles, what the Three Pashas had tried to do to the Ottoman Empire: cleanse it. He wanted to wipe away everything that he didn't like, and the Pashas may as well have been his heroes. The Jews were the Armenians of Germany, and Hitler would launch, on an utterly terrifying scale, the same atrocities the Pashas had committed.

By this time, Armenia had faded from the consciousness of the world, and the fact that Turkey had rebuilt its entire economy on the property that had been stolen from dead or deported Armenians had been allowed to slip away quietly and without contest. In fact, Hitler himself, as he prepared to launch the Holocaust, used the forgetfulness of the global conscience to excuse away the terrible things he was about to do. "Who remembers Armenia?" he asked, implying that even though the genocide had taken place less than thirty years ago, it had already been forgotten by most of the world.

But not everyone had forgotten. Following in the footsteps of his compatriot Wegner, a German writer and activist named Raphael Lemkin would be the first to name the terrible things that he saw occurring in the world around him. Lemkin wrote about the things that had been done to the Armenians—first in the ordinary letters of the laws that had stripped them of their rights and then, brutally, in the savage treatment that had been inflicted upon them—and drew highly unpopular parallels between the massacres in Armenia and the Holocaust of the Jews. It was Lemkin who would give this atrocity a name. He called it "genocide," and the world would finally have something to define the awful killings of an entire race.

The very term "genocide" would prove as controversial as Lemkin's opinions of it. In Nazi Germany, to be vociferously in opposition to the Fatherland and its dictator was to court disaster. Armin Wegner had not allowed fear to silence him; in 1933, he had written an open angry letter to Hitler denouncing his treatment of the Jews, using the strong words, "There is no Fatherland without Justice!"

The Gestapo came for Wegner and tortured him, and the great activist would go on to suffer alongside those same Jews in those same concentration camps, witnessing the terrible treatment of them firsthand before he was released before WWII broke out and fled the country. But despite what had happened to Wegner, Lemkin would continue to protest that what had happened to the Armenians was wrong and what was happening to the Jews was even worse. With his life in peril, Lemkin succeeded in leaving Germany to work with Americans in Washington, D. C., in 1942. It was here that he wrote his *Axis Rule in Occupied Europe*, and the word "genocide" first entered the world's vocabulary.

It was a word that Lemkin would use to good effect, too. He worked closely on the Nuremberg trials, where he first heard that nearly fifty members of his immediate family had been killed in the genocide for which he was prosecuting the Germans (Lemkin himself was Jewish). Of course, many of the most important perpetrators of the Holocaust had committed suicide before the trials. Adolf Hitler, Heinrich Himmler, and Robert Ley were among them.

Once the Nuremberg trials were over, however, the word "genocide" could not be put to rest. The world began to wonder where else genocide had been committed, and Armenia was the most recent. Armenians themselves were quick to adopt the term and just as quick to demand justice for what had been done to them.

The United Nations followed in 1948, acknowledging that what had happened in Armenia was a crime against humanity, even though by then there was almost no one left to actually prosecute for it—Operation Nemesis had made sure of that. By 1985, the UN officially recognized the events in Armenia as a genocide. Much of this is due to lobbying by Cyprus; it had legally recognized the genocide by 1975, and in the modern day, actually denying the genocide is a crime in Cyprus. The very first country, however, to recognize the genocide was Uruguay, which has had an Armenian population since the early 19th century.

One by one, countries across the globe have followed in recognizing the suffering of the Armenian people. Argentina, Belgium, Canada, France, Greece, Lebanon, and Russia all recognized the genocide in the 1990s; Chile, Germany, Italy, Lithuania, the Netherlands, Poland, Slovakia, Switzerland, the Holy See, and Venezuela followed suit in the early 2000s. There are a few nations, however, that have not yet made their respect for the Armenians' suffering official. Among them are the United States (although 49 out of 50 states do recognize the genocide) and the United Kingdom. Both of these countries have likely done so out of fear of angering Turkey because, of course, no country is louder in denying that the genocide ever happened than Turkey itself.

A simple number easily summarizes Turkey's stance on the genocide: 300,000. This is the number of Armenians that Turkey officially recognizes as having been killed in the genocide. This more or less assumes that about one million Armenians simply disappeared into thin air during the First World War, considering that around two million Armenians lived in the Ottoman Empire before the war, and only about 400,000 were left afterward. Historians and genocide scholars are in agreement all over the world that the figure Turkey stands by is grossly inaccurate.

Another Turkish stance on the genocide is that it was justified by the acts of the Armenians during the First World War. While it is true that Armenian rebels betrayed the Ottomans to Russia, igniting a revolt that claimed Turkish lives, it is unlikely that the thousands of women and children thrown overboard in the Black Sea at the command of the Butcher of Trebizond were in any way involved with any kind of rebellion.

Turkey similarly denies the fact that Greeks and Assyrians, who also suffered the same awful mistreatment as the Armenians during the First World War, were victims of genocide during the Ottoman era. The "Turkification" that the Young Turks began more than a hundred years ago is still in force to the modern day. Motives for denying the genocide are likely rooted in fears that to recognize the genocide would mean making reparations to the descendants of its victims—and considering that much of the modern Turkish economy depends on the burgeoning middle class, that might be disastrous for the country. There were very few middle-class Turks before the genocide; much of today's middle class started out as menial laborers who rose in the social ranks because of buying cheap Armenian properties.

The Turkish denial of the Armenian Genocide is so severe that merely mentioning the genocide in Turkey is a crime. However, pressure from the rest of the world to mend fences with Armenia may be starting to nudge Turkey toward recognition of what its hulking ancestor, the Ottoman Empire, has done. There is hope that, someday, Turkey will be able to acknowledge its mistakes, enabling the Turks and the Armenians alive today to move forward.

# Chapter 14 – Fighting for Freedom

Mount Ararat towers over the city of Yerevan, capital of modern-day Armenia
*https://commons.wikimedia.org/w/index.php?curid=1282772*

In the wake of World War I, the Ottoman Empire's collapse left a power vacuum in the territories it had once oppressed, and the Armenians were finally able to take advantage of that vacuum.

For centuries, Armenia was passed back and forth from one ambitious empire to the other. Rome, Persia, the Ottomans—they had all been controlling the little country and its people for generations upon generations. But the end of WWI saw independence being given to colonies all over the world, and Armenia was no exception. Under pressure from the Allies and still focusing on bringing together the new Republic of Turkey, Atatürk had to watch as the borders of the once-great empire splintered. One of those splinters was formally established on May 28th, 1918, as the Republic of Armenia.

Those Armenians who had survived and stayed in their ancestral homeland could hardly believe it. They were free at last. No longer would they be harshly taxed simply because they worshiped differently; no longer would they face massacre after massacre. As the genocide still continued within the borders of Turkey, a great flight of refugees started to pour from Turkey into Armenia. While these refugees were grateful to have finally found a place that was supposed to be their safe home, things did not bode well for the new little republic. Most of its population was crippled by the terrible genocide that had just taken place. With three out of every four Armenians in the Ottoman Empire killed during the darkness of the preceding years, practically every Armenian had either witnessed these atrocities, suffered through some of them, or lost someone they loved to them. The genocide was all-encompassing; it affected everyone, and the nation was brokenhearted after seeing the wholesale destruction of its people.

Knowing this, multiple smaller countries—themselves fragments of the shattered empire—saw Armenia as a target. Only a few weeks after the Republic of Armenia was established, it found itself under fire from neighboring Georgia over provinces on the border. Georgia was surprised to see the vehemence with which the Armenians resisted any of their lands being taken. Their people had been robbed of too much and for far too long, and they fought back with a spirit that was surprising considering what they had just suffered.

Azerbaijan was another antagonist of Armenia's bid to carve out its independence. Closely allied with Turkey—its culture and religion mirroring its intimidating neighbor —Azerbaijan took advantage of the fact that Armenia's borders had not yet been officially drawn. It laid claim to several areas of Armenia, including the capital, Yerevan, in the shadow of Mount Ararat. Despite British intervention, a diplomatic solution was never reached. Azerbaijan invaded the Armenian borders determined to claim the land it saw as belonging rightfully to the Azerbaijani, but its claim would never be successful. Once again, despite the horrors that they had just suffered, the Armenians pushed back. By 1920, the Azerbaijani had been chased back to their own country, and Armenia seemed to be finding its feet at last.

The Treaty of Sèvres was signed in August 1920 between the Allies and the Ottoman Empire. One of its conditions was to define the borders of Armenia and also for all of the involved parties to recognize it as a fully independent state. The Ottoman Empire begrudgingly did so under its last sultan, but its recognition of its most hated enemy would not last for very long. Only a month later, under Atatürk, Turkey invaded Armenia on a scale that even these spirited people could not stand against.

By November, two-thirds of Armenia was under Turkish control. And by December, that control had been transferred once again. Just as Armenia had fallen victim to the Roman Empire and to Alexander the Great, it was now wheat before the scythe of the world's newest rising empire, the Soviet Union. Armenia became the Armenian Soviet

Socialist Republic, and it would remain under the control of the Soviets for the next seven decades.

When the USSR crumbled in 1991, Armenia found itself free at last, but like many countries that had been deeply dependent on the Soviet Union, it was mostly free to starve to death. Armenia had been so deeply dependent on the USSR, particularly for fuel, that its citizens found themselves practically without electricity. In fact, they had to survive on only four hours of power per day. In the cold mountains of Armenia, it wasn't enough; even almost thirty years later, the country is still trying to recover from the deforestation and overfishing that took place as a starving people tried to make their way through the winter.

But Armenians had seen worse than this. It was seventy years after the genocide had ended, yet the terrible events were still alive in memories and in the gaping holes that had been ripped in family trees. They survived the darkness and rebuilt their country practically from scratch, and Armenia was declared, once again, to be an independent republic. Its first democratic elections held on October 16th, 1991. Despite considerable corruption and natural disasters that rocked the country, Armenia entered the 21st century as a nation that was slowly rising from the ashes.

Rigged elections peppered the first few decades of Armenian independence. Perhaps the most corrupt of the Armenian presidents was Robert Kocharyan, the second president of Armenia. Kocharyan should never have been president in the first place; he had not been an Armenian citizen for long enough according to his own constitution. Nonetheless, he succeeded in rigging the election so that he could take power and become the president of Armenia in 1998.

Kocharyan's main rival, Karen Demirchyan, was more popular with the people. He held the role of Parliament Speaker during Kocharyan's presidency, and together with the prime minister, Vazgen Sargsyan, he worked to sideline Kocharyan from the political scene as much as possible. Within a year, Armenian politics were largely in the hands of Demirchyan and Sargsyan, with Kocharyan reduced to something of a figurehead.

Until one fateful day in October 1999, when both of Kocharyan's rivals would conveniently be removed from the scene entirely.

* * * *

Parliament was in session, and Kocharyan was getting tired of hearing the voices of his two rivals drone on and on. They had all but seized control of the country, pushing Kocharyan to the sidelines even though he held the title of president. Some would argue that in doing so, Demirchyan and Sargsyan were helping Armenia on the road to true democracy and independence as a nation that was still fumbling for footing after centuries of rule by one greedy empire after another. It certainly appears as though Sargsyan was not corrupt or at least not as corrupt as his counterpart, Kocharyan. And some would not argue. Some would just pick up AK-47s, walk into Parliament, and open fire.

On October 27th, 1999, five gunmen did exactly that. Led by a former ARF member, they stormed the National Assembly building armed with machine guns. Journalists and politicians scattered for cover among the benches in the parliamentary building as the men headed straight for their target: the prime minister, Vazgen Sargsyan. They raised their voices so that the journalists could hear every word of their exchange.

It was Nairi Hunanyan, the leader of the group, who approached Sargsyan first with a gun aimed for him and a slew of accusations. Hunanyan called Sargsyan corrupt and a profiteer. His words as he strode up to the prime minister were chilling.

"Enough of drinking our blood!" he cried, seized by the fervor of bloodlust and what he saw as patriotism.

Sargsyan's reply was unruffled by the barrel of the machine gun leveled at his chest. "Everything is being done for you," he said, "and the future of your children."

After that, Hunanyan let his bullets do the talking. He poured rounds into Sargsyan at point-blank range, killing him instantly, and his fellow terrorists opened fire. By the time the bullets had stopped flying, eight politicians were dead, Sargsyan and Demirchyan among them. President Robert Kocharyan, whom the terrorists identified as being the leader that Armenia truly needed, was untouched.

This and other facts—especially the four-year trial that followed the shootings, which were handled so lackadaisically that the Armenian public could not help but speculate whether the government was dragging its feet in a bid to hide something—would lead to Robert Kocharyan becoming the main suspect that the Armenian people believed had instigated the shootings. It had certainly strengthened his position in Parliament; for the next ten years, Kocharyan's authoritarian rule would see Armenia's slow side away from democracy and into just another state ruled by a selfish dictator. Armenians protested, of course. They had survived far too much to suffer oppression from one of their own. When Levon Ter-Petrosyan, who had been the first president of Armenia, announced his candidacy in the 2008 elections, the protests took a turn for the violent. Ter-Petrosyan had proven to be something of a dictator in his seven years as president from 1991 to 1998, and he was widely accused of having rigged the 1996 elections. Trying to avoid yet another rigged election, protesters in Yerevan turned violent and started looting and attacking authorities. While the police at first tried to break things up using non-lethal methods, the situation escalated, and the military was called into Yerevan. By the time the violence was over, ten protesters had been killed. Their supporters argued that the authorities had been looking for a reason to open fire on them.

Ter-Petrosyan did not win the elections; instead, Serzh Sargsyan became president, along with a slew of promises that he would be different. Over the next ten years, it became evident that Sargsyan had little intention of making good on his promises. Going directly against what he had said before his presidency, he made himself prime minister as well as the president in 2018, amassing a dangerous amount of power. In fact, the people feared that Sargsyan would be able to stay in power for life.

By 2018, a wave of revolution was sweeping across the Middle East, and discontent peaked in Armenia. Yet memories of the bloodshed in 2008 forced the people to reconsider their tactics. Looting and violence were not going to be the answer; instead, nationwide protests would have to be truly peaceful. And to achieve this, a politician named Nikol Pashinyan knew that the people needed a leader.

Pashinyan was a nobody, a journalist who led a puny opposition party that barely featured on the radar of the Armenian people. But the nation needed a leader, someone who was brave enough to walk forward into the future, and at the end of March 2018, Pashinyan became that person. He announced that he was going to walk the 120 miles from the city of Gyumri to Yerevan, peacefully protesting Sergsyan's new appointment as prime minister.

When he set out from Gyumri, a handful of curious journalists were trailing after him. But when he reached Yerevan more than two weeks later, the streets were flooded with crowds of Armenians. They had painted faces and carried Armenian flags; they were laughing and shouting and cheering their slogans, and they had rallied around an ordinary-looking middle-aged man in a khaki shirt and cap. Pashinyan proceeded to lead what is now known as the "Velvet Revolution," an entirely peaceful protest and general strike that resulted in no deaths. The streets were closed, workers went on strike, but there were no casualties. There was no violence. Photographs show children on their parents' shoulders, holding up the flag of their people. In fact, it was downright civilized; Pashinyan asked his protesters to get off the street by ten in the evening. It was a protest with a bedtime.

When Sargsyan tried to get the army involved, even that failed. The soldiers laid down their weapons and joined the protest, and Sargsyan knew that he had been beaten. He resigned his post on April 23$^{rd}$, after having kept Pashinyan briefly in prison. A short while later, Pashinyan's party was elected, and he became the president of Armenia.

Today, Armenia keeps on taking small steps toward becoming a whole and hopeful nation. This is a nation that survived genocide yet staged a revolution without any violence and without any support from any of the "big brother" powers—like the E.U., the U.S., and Russia. Like its culture, like its religion, like its indomitable spirit, the Velvet Revolution was nothing if not one thing:

It was uniquely Armenian.

# Conclusion

One hundred years ago, Armenia was a name on the lips and hearts of America. Children who wouldn't finish their food were told to eat up because there were starving children in Armenia; missionaries were sent there, and the well-meaning donated to ACASR's cause, as the genocide—even though it could not yet be called by that name—became the cause of the day.

Today, however, newspaper articles published for an American audience have to clarify where Armenia even is. Even in Hitler's time, the genocide had already been forgotten by the conscience of the world.

Armenians, however, do not forget—not in the spirit with which they continue to move forward within their own mother country, and not in the vibrant and thriving diaspora communities that popped up all over the world in the trembling wake of the genocide.

All over the world—from Australia to France to Brazil to the U.S. and back again—Armenians have made their homes in foreign countries, continuing with their lives after fleeing from the wrath of the Turks.

These days, the firsthand accounts of the genocide are stories passed down from great-grandparents. But many parts of Armenian culture are still a part of the lives of those who escaped the genocide. Armenian Americans could visit France and find food being served there by people who look like them, food that their parents or grandparents might have cooked in their own homes. There seems to be a link running through all Armenians, regardless of where they come from, a mutual recognition of who they are despite what they have endured.

Eight million Armenians today live in the various diaspora communities, the largest of these being in the United States (specifically Los Angeles) and the Krasnodar region of Russia. The Ottoman attempt to exterminate the Armenians once and for all could not have failed more spectacularly, although many regions of ancient Armenia, which are now no longer part of the modern Republic of Armenia, are totally devoid of ethnic Armenians.

Yet even though Armenia continues to lobby for Turkish recognition of the genocide, many Armenians are ready to put the past behind them and stride into the future, bringing with them not the bitterness of what their ancestors endured but rather the fearless spirit that allowed them to survive. An Armenian-American photojournalist, Scout Tufankjian, who has devoted much of her life to photographing people in the various diaspora communities, said it best.

"We are so much more than the genocide. We have survived. And we have thrived."

# Here's another book by Captivating History that you might like

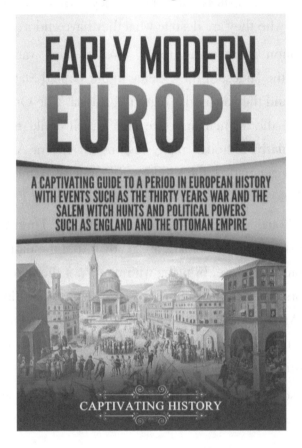

# Free Bonus from Captivating History (Available for a Limited time)

Hi History Lovers!

Now you have a chance to join our exclusive history list so you can get your first history ebook for free as well as discounts and a potential to get more history books for free! Simply visit the link below to join.

Captivatinghistory.com/ebook

Also, make sure to follow us on Facebook, Twitter and Youtube by searching for Captivating History.

# Sources

http://100years100facts.com/facts/garden-eden-traditions-located-armenia/

https://www.peopleofar.com/2013/12/02/armenia-the-forgotten-paradise/

https://bible.knowing-jesus.com/Genesis/2/type/kjv

https://www.thevintagenews.com/2019/05/08/areni-1/

https://www.thevintagenews.com/2017/06/02/the-areni-1-shoe-the-oldest-leather-shoe-in-the-world-was-found-in-a-cave-in-armenia/

https://www.atlasobscura.com/places/areni-1-cave-complex

https://www.ancient.eu/Areni_Cave/

https://www.ancient.eu/Tushpa/

https://www.livius.org/articles/place/tuspa-van/

https://www.christianity.com/church/denominations/discover-the-assyrians-10-things-to-know-about-their-history-faith.html

https://books.google.co.za/books?id=OR_PHoKZ6ycC&pg=PA67&lpg=PA67&dq=aramu+urartu&source=bl&ots=e_ZxonHPrQ&sig=ACfU3U36PTCJ0iihLc2ZZ8sNKG10USso3A&hl=en&sa=X&ved=2ahUKEwi5qMfC_-bkAhVFXRUIHfbXDikQ6AEwEXoECAwQAQ#v=onepage&q=aramu%20urartu&f=false

https://tamarnajarian.wordpress.com/2012/02/17/arame-king-of-urartu/

https://www.ancient.eu/Urartu_Civilization/

https://www.degruyter.com/view/j/jah.2016.4.issue-1/jah-2015-0024/jah-2015-0024.xml

http://bronze-age-towns.over-blog.com/2016/12/musri-or-musasir-the-city-of-mudjesir.html

https://www.britannica.com/place/Urartu

https://www.livius.org/articles/people/medes/

https://www.britannica.com/place/Media-ancient-region-Iran

https://www.ancient.eu/Cyrus_the_Great/

https://www.nationalgeographic.com/culture/people/reference/cyrus-the-great/

https://www.history.com/topics/religion/zoroastrianism

https://www.youtube.com/watch?v=lP5RqosiYQA

https://www.ancient-origins.net/history-famous-people/mithridates-vi-pontus-poison-king-pontus-and-aggravation-rome-005907

https://www.thoughtco.com/pompey-the-great-pompeius-magnus-112662

https://www.livius.org/articles/person/tigranes-ii/

https://www.ancient.eu/Tigranes_the_Great/

https://www.britannica.com/biography/Lucius-Licinius-Lucullus

https://www.britannica.com/biography/Tigranes-II-the-Great

https://www.ancient-origins.net/history/rise-and-fall-tigranes-great-king-armenia-002815

https://www.ancient.eu/pompey/

https://www.britannica.com/biography/Vonones-I

https://www.britannica.com/biography/Artavasdes-II

https://www.historynet.com/mark-antonys-persian-campaign.htm

https://www.encyclopedia.com/religion/encyclopedias-almanacs-transcripts-and-maps/tiridates-iii-armenian-king


https://www.ancient-origins.net/history-famous-people/diocletian-0010984?utm_source=feedburner&utm_medium=feed&utm_campaign=Feed%3A+AncientOrigins+%28Ancient+Origins%29

https://www.christianity.com/church/church-history/timeline/1-300/yield-or-suffer-said-diocletian-11629633.html

https://allinnet.info/news/the-goddess-of-love-and-fertility-anahit-ancient-armenia-preface/

https://www.ancient.eu/article/801/the-early-christianization-of-armenia/

http://www.iranchamber.com/history/parthians/parthians.php

http://factsanddetails.com/central-asia/Central_Asian_Topics/sub8_8a/entry-4502.html#chapter-10

https://www.livius.org/articles/person/vologases-iv/

https://www.historynet.com/romes-parthian-war-d-161-166.htm

https://www.ancient.eu/armenia/

https://www.britannica.com/biography/Saint-Mesrop-Mashtots

https://www.thevintagenews.com/2017/01/31/mesrop-mashtots-plight-for-the-armenian-alphabet-and-language/

https://www.britannica.com/topic/Armenian-language

https://armeniadiscovery.com/en/articles/mesrop-mashtots-the-creator-of-the-armenian-alphabet

https://www.deseret.com/2018/3/16/20641780/armenia-the-first-christian-nation

https://www.ancient.eu/Arsacid_Dynasty_of_Armenia/

https://www.thoughtco.com/war-elephants-in-asian-history-195817

https://www.ancient-origins.net/history/war-elephants-military-tanks-ancient-world-009967

https://www.ancient-origins.net/history/immortals-elite-army-persian-empire-never-grew-weak-002321

https://www.ancient.eu/image/8231/battle-of-avarayr/

https://armenianchurch.us/essential_grid/st-vartan-and-the-battle-of-avarayr/

https://www.britannica.com/biography/Saint-Vardan-Mamikonian#ref1078407

https://www.livius.org/articles/person/heraclius/

https://www.ancient-origins.net/history-famous-people/heraclius-0011027

https://www.ancient.eu/article/1207/byzantine-armenian-relations/

https://www.britannica.com/biography/Maurice-Byzantine-emperor

https://www.encyclopedia.com/religion/encyclopedias-almanacs-transcripts-and-maps/maurice-byzantine-emperor

https://www.livius.org/articles/person/phocas/

https://www.britannica.com/biography/Phocas

http://www.fsmitha.com/h3/islam04.htm

https://www.ancient.eu/Dvin/

https://www.history.com/topics/religion/islam

http://www.armenian-history.com/Nyuter/HISTORY/middle%20ages/Armenia_%20in_7th_and_%208th_centuries.htm

https://www.peopleofar.com/2019/01/05/the-forgotten-kingdom-bagratid-armenia/

https://www.peopleofar.com/2014/01/13/ani-city-of-1001-churches-2/

---

https://www.peopleofar.com/2012/01/28/armenian-crusaders/

https://www.medievalists.net/2011/07/the-crusaders-through-armenian-eyes/

https://www.thoughtco.com/who-were-the-seljuks-195399

https://www.ancient.eu/First_Crusade/

http://historyofarmenia.org/2017/04/23/mongols-invade-armenia/

https://www.britannica.com/biography/Levon-I

https://allinnet.info/history/levon-the-great-king-of-cilicia-the-armenian-rubenid-dynasty/

https://www.panorama.am/en/news/2016/03/07/Aris-Ghazinyan/1539066

https://www.bbc.com/news/magazine-20538810

https://www.thoughtco.com/timur-or-tamerlane-195675

https://www.britannica.com/biography/Timur

https://www.britannica.com/place/Little-Armenia

https://www.thoughtco.com/who-were-the-mamluks-195371

https://www.nationalgeographic.com/culture/people/reference/mongols/

https://www.thoughtco.com/genghis-khan-195669

https://www.theguardian.com/world/2015/apr/24/armenian-genocide-survivors-stories-my-dreams-cannot-mourn

https://www.armenian-genocide.org/adana.html

https://www.britannica.com/topic/Hamidian-massacres

https://www.history.com/topics/world-war-i/armenian-genocide

http://www.armeniapedia.org/wiki/Armenian_Soviet_Socialist_Republic

https://mirrorspectator.com/2018/05/24/the-battle-of-sardarapat-and-its-aftermath/

http://historyofarmenia.org/2017/05/28/battle-sardarabad-birth-new-nation/

http://www.panarmenian.net/eng/details/179324/

https://www.youtube.com/watch?v=cQanB0lR81A

https://www.azatutyun.am/a/26806241.html

https://www.rferl.org/a/armenians-speak-one-year-on-from-revolution/29898637.html

https://www.tandfonline.com/doi/abs/10.1080/10999922.2019.1581042?af=R&journalCode=mpin20

https://griffithreview.atavist.com/life-after-genocide

https://www.britannica.com/place/Armenia/The-marzpans

http://www.newadvent.org/cathen/07023a.htm

https://www.ancient.eu/Saint_Gregory_the_Illuminator/

https://www.plough.com/en/topics/culture/music/how-christianity-came-to-armenia

http://armeniancenters.com/armenian-history-summary/

https://greekcitytimes.com/2019/05/29/may-29-1453-the-fall-of-constantinople/

http://www.thenagain.info/WebChron/EastEurope/FallConstantin.html

https://www.britannica.com/event/Fall-of-Constantinople-1453

http://www.ottomansouvenir.com/more_on_ottoman_empire.htm

https://www.historyextra.com/period/medieval/6-things-you-probably-didnt-know-about-the-ottoman-empire/

https://www.history.com/topics/middle-east/ottoman-empire

https://www.huffpost.com/entry/the-armenian-question-a-s_b_185846?guccounter=1&guce_referrer=aHR0cHM6Ly93d3cuZ29vZ2xlLmNvbS88&guce_referrer_sig=AQAAAFqf_0Uld7R_ww1u-3zmtWUOsoPjAryYEpO2aC_4te3C9SFZBCyttdNx0_VwqqFGYGCk1vQZ2kezzQDqmyOxDP7Ndn51OQw7LN7qbdcaCpqVMxM_hsVTpQNqQ1bvMU2yn4ssVYWOo3fvR8UPP4eb93MTedg9J2Im-Zn6CCoyxSfE

http://www.arabnews.com/node/1487201/middle-east

https://www.newworldencyclopedia.org/entry/Abdul_Hamid_II

https://biography.yourdictionary.com/abdul-hamid-ii

https://www.armenian-genocide.org/hamidian.html

https://journals.openedition.org/eac/1641

https://theamericanmag.com/queen-please-help/

https://www.geni.com/people/Rev-Crosby-Wheeler-D-D/6000000074716927124

http://www.hurriyetdailynews.com/opinion/william-armstrong/the-1909-massacres-of-armenians-in-adana-96825

https://www.newworldencyclopedia.org/entry/Young_Turk_Revolution

https://ipfs.io/ipfs/QmXoypizjW3WknFjJnKLwHCnL72vedxjQkDDP1mXWo6uco/wiki/Ahmed_Niyazi_Bey.html

https://www.thoughtco.com/causes-that-led-to-world-war-i-105515

https://medium.com/@dhireshnathwani/what-was-the-most-significant-cause-of-world-war-one-ww1-74bb9e815e37

https://www.history.com/topics/world-war-i/world-war-i-history#section_2

http://www.thenagain.info/WebChron/EastEurope/TurkeyCentral.html

https://nzhistory.govt.nz/war/ottoman-empire/enters-the-war

https://www.britannica.com/topic/Balkan-Wars

https://www.hmd.org.uk/resource/24-april-1915-deportation-of-armenian-intellectuals/

https://www.cmi.no/news/1531-100-years-since-the-deportation

http://chilingirianquartet.co.uk/armenian-komitas-songs/

https://www.britannica.com/biography/Komitas

https://www.theguardian.com/music/2011/apr/21/komitas-vardapet-folk-music-armenia

https://www.allthelyrics.com/forum/showthread.php?t=50631

http://ww1blog.osborneink.com/?p=7328

https://www.historynet.com/the-defense-of-van.htm

https://www.armenian-genocide.org/wegnerbio.html

https://www.yadvashem.org/righteous/stories/wegner.html

http://100years100facts.com/facts/armin-wegner-took-pictures-saw-1915/

https://www.huffpost.com/entry/armenian-genocide-controversy_n_7121008

http://www.armin.am/armeniansgenocide/en/Encyclopedia_Of_armenian_genocide_death_march

https://encyclopedia.ushmm.org/content/en/article/the-armenian-genocide-1915-16-in-depth

https://www.irishtimes.com/culture/books/armin-wegner-the-german-who-stood-up-to-genocide-of-both-armenians-and-jews-1.2201998

http://www.genocide1915.org/bildgalleri_wegner.html

https://www.ushmm.org/information/exhibitions/online-exhibitions/special-focus/armenia/testimonies

https://qz.com/1310263/americas-extraordinary-history-with-armenian-refugees/

https://archive.nytimes.com/www.nytimes.com/ref/timestopics/topics_armenian
genocide.html?mcubz=0

https://books.google.co.za/books?id=h7ZIDwAAQBAJ&pg=PA205&lpg=PA2
05&dq=ali+suad+bey&source=bl&ots=NmgsuKPjkK&sig=ACfU3U2HqZIgVE
q44BpBp1ctKP0RnXom2w&hl=en&sa=X&ved=2ahUKEwiLhbeSmbTkAhU
EKewKHVOoAq8Q6AEwBnoECAgQAQ#v=onepage&q=ali%20suad%20bey
&f=false

https://www.armenian-genocide.org/1915-3.html

https://www.quora.com/How-was-the-Armenian-Genocide-carried-out

https://books.google.co.za/books?id=McsxDwAAQBAJ&pg=PA655&lpg=PA6
55&dq=%22ali+suad+bey%22&source=bl&ots=vD6zZ2gmlh&sig=ACfU3U1tn
CKZMsoAF1Clbyzv4GjR7tWOnA&hl=en&sa=X&ved=2ahUKEwjt49PUmbT
kAhWGvKQKHXGKB9QQ6AEwBnoECAgQAQ#v=onepage&q=%22ali%2
0suad%20bey%22&f=false

https://www.catholiceducation.org/en/controversy/persecution/who-remembers-the-armenians.html

https://hyetert.org/2012/03/29/the-armenian-genocide-and-the-extraordinary-role-of-deir-zor-governor-zeki-bey/

https://www.armenian-history.com/Nyuter/HISTORY/ARMENIA20/armenian_genocide.htm

http://www.uacla.com/eitan-belkind.html

http://www.gen-mus.co.il/en/person/?id=2493

https://www.jewishvirtuallibrary.org/the-nili-spy-ring

https://www.medicinenet.com/typhus/article.htm

http://www.noravank.am/eng/issues/detail.php?ELEMENT_ID=3718

https://armenianweekly.com/2016/05/31/ruben-heryan/

https://www.britannica.com/biography/Ahmed-Riza

http://100years100facts.com/facts/turkeys-economy-today-based-part-confiscated-armenian-property/

https://mirrorspectator.com/2018/04/19/commemorating-genocide-the-role-of-property-seizure-in-the-armenian-genocide-and-its-aftermath/

https://encyclopedia.ushmm.org/content/en/article/the-armenian-genocide-1915-16-overview

https://www.bbc.co.uk/bitesize/articles/zkb86v4

https://www.history.com/this-day-in-history/world-war-i-ends

https://www.history.com/topics/middle-east/ottoman-empire#section_9

https://nzhistory.govt.nz/war/ottoman-empire/at-war

https://www.volkansadventures.com/history/turkey-first-world-war-armistice-mudros/

https://www.dailysabah.com/feature/2018/10/30/the-armistice-that-spelled-the-end-of-the-ottoman-empire

https://www.iwm.org.uk/history/9-reasons-why-gallipoli-was-one-of-the-worst-fighting-fronts-of-the-first-world-war

https://www.history.com/topics/world-war-i/battle-of-gallipoli-1

http://endgenocide.org/the-armenian-genocide-where-is-justice/

https://www.oxfordscholarship.com/view/10.1093/acprof:oso/9780199671144.001.0001/acprof-9780199671144-chapter-4

https://ayfwest.org/news/the-constantinople-war-crimes-trials-the-legal-response-to-the-armenian-genocide/

https://www.history.com/topics/middle-east/kemal-ataturk#section_2

http://www.armeniapedia.org/wiki/The_Trial_of_Soghomon_Tehlirian

http://100years100facts.com/facts/talaat-pasha-assassinated-berlin-15th-march-1921/

https://www.independent.co.uk/voices/robert-fisk-armenian-genocide-conversation-son-of-soghomon-tehlirian-mehmet-talaat-pasha-a7091951.html

https://www.huffpost.com/entry/erics-bogosians-operation_b_7097268

https://www.spectator.co.uk/2015/06/the-long-shadow-of-genocide-armenias-vengeance-years/

https://www.telegraph.co.uk/news/worldnews/europe/turkey/11373115/Amal-Clooneys-latest-case-Why-Turkey-wont-talk-about-the-Armenian-genocide.html

https://eurasianet.org/turks-commemorate-armenian-genocide-despite-taboos

http://www.genocidewatch.org/aboutus/thecostofdenial.html

https://ahvalnews.com/armenian-genocide/turkey-pays-price-denying-armenian-genocide

https://encyclopedia.ushmm.org/content/en/article/international-military-tribunal-at-nuremberg

https://www.operationnemesis.com/

https://www.nytimes.com/2015/04/19/books/review/19bkr-kanon.t.html

https://www.bbc.com/news/world-europe-43948181

https://www.thenation.com/article/armenia-revolution-elections/

https://narcokarabakh.net/en/profiles/rkocharyan

https://www.rferl.org/a/Ten_Years_Later_Deadly_Shooting_In_Armenian_Parliament_Still_Echoes/1862158.html

https://www.nytimes.com/2008/03/02/world/europe/02armenia.html

http://www.littlearmenia.com/html/little_armenia/armenian_history.asp

https://www.advantour.com/armenia/history.htm

http://www.auschwitz.dk/holofaq.htm

https://www.dw.com/en/holocaust-remembrance-in-germany-a-changing-culture/a-47203540

https://journals.openedition.org/eac/565?lang=en

https://www.rferl.org/a/armenia-society/26935197.html

https://www.ft.com/content/2e2f38b0-e7a1-11e8-8a85-04b8afea6ea3

Made in United States
Troutdale, OR
07/19/2024

21395104R00141